· Véronique Enginger ·

Retro Cross Stitch

500 PATTERNS

French Charm for Your
Stitchwork

4880 Lower Valley Road • Atglen, PA 19310

Originally published as *Point de Croix Rétro* © 2016 by Éditions Mango Pratique, Paris. Translated from the French by Omicron Language Solutions, LLC.

Library of Congress Control Number: 2017951910

Cover design by Molly Shields
Production design by Danielle D. Farmer

Editorial director: Tatiana Delesalle
Editing: Mélanie Jean
Artistic director: Chloé Eve
Photos: Fabrice Besse
Design: Sonia Roy
Photos and design (except for "Chocolate, Tea, Coffee"): Franck Schmitt
Layout: Vincent Fraboulet
Production: Sabine Marioni

Type set in Honey Script/Adobe Garamond Pro/ParisineClair/DIN

ISBN: 978-0-7643-5479-3
Printed in China

Published by Schiffer Publishing, Ltd.
4880 Lower Valley Road
Atglen, PA 19310
Phone: (610) 593-1777; Fax: (610) 593-2002
E-mail: Info@schifferbooks.com
Web: www.schifferbooks.com

For our complete selection of fine books on this and related subjects, please visit our website at www.schifferbooks.com. You may also write for a free catalog.

Schiffer Publishing's titles are available at special discounts for bulk purchases for sales promotions or premiums. Special editions, including personalized covers, corporate imprints, and excerpts, can be created in large quantities for special needs. For more information, contact the publisher.

We are always looking for people to write books on new and related subjects. If you have an idea for a book, please contact us at proposals@schifferbooks.com.

Other Schiffer Books on Related Subjects:

Inspiration Kantha: Creative Stitchery and Quilting with Asia's Ancient Technique, Anna Hergert, ISBN 978-0-7643-5357-4

The Art of Weaving a Life: A Framework to Expand and Strengthen Your Personal Vision, Susan Barrett Merrill, ISBN 978-0-7643-5264-5

The Little Guide to Mastering Your Sewing Machine: All the Sewing Basics, Plus 15 Step-by-Step Projects, Sylvie Blondeau, ISBN 978-0-7643-4970-6

Contents

Basic Information

⸬ Cross Stitch

Cross stitch is easy. It's composed of two crossing slanted stitches. They can be done individually or continuously (see the diagram below).

When doing individual cross stitches, always finish one before starting on another. Your work will be more even.

The best type of thread for cross stitch is called floss. Made up of six cotton strands, it can be divided into fewer strands depending on the fabric's mesh size and the needs of the design. On each pattern, you'll see the color numbers for DMC brand cotton floss.

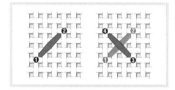

Individual cross stitch   Continuous cross stitch

Other Stitches

The half cross stitch, or tapestry stitch, is nothing more than a cross stitch with only one slanting stitch. It allows you to reduce the intensity of a color and to create shadow on a background.

The quarter cross stitch lets you create details that are impossible to do with a cross stitch.

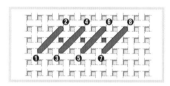

Half cross stitch or
tapestry stitch

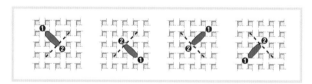

Quarter cross stitch

The three-quarter cross stitch is made up of a half stitch and a quarter stitch. It too helps with adding detail, including curves, to designs.

All three of these stitches are symbolized on the chart in the same way: with a half-square. ◪, ◨, ◩, ◧. It's up to you to choose the type of stitch that works best for the situation.

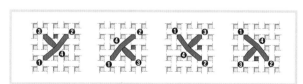

Three-quarter cross stitch

The back stitch, also called the straight stitch, is ideal for bordering a motif, underlining a certain part, or showing a detail, just the way a line drawn with a pencil would. It is done after the entire cross stitch design is completely finished. Usually the back stitch is done with fewer strands than the cross stitch, and most of the time in a color that's a shade darker. Depending on what result you want, you can follow the contours of the crosses, lengthen the stitches, or work diagonally. On the charts, the back stitches are represented by continuous lines.

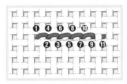

Back stitching on each thread of the canvas

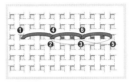

Long back stitch

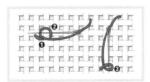

French knot

The French knot is used, for example, for a character's eyes or a flower's stamens, where a cross would be too big. It is indicated on the charts with a small circle ●.

Accessories

Needle

The tapestry needle is used for cross stitching. It has a rounded tip and the eye is larger than a sewing needle's. Its rounded tip helps avoid damage to the canvas mesh, and the larger eye allows for the threading of thicker or multiple strands. The most common sizes are numbered 18 to 28. The higher the size number, the thinner the needle. A number 26 size needle is perfect for working with one strand, but you will need a size 24 needle when working with two or three strands. The mesh size you're working with also helps determine the best needle size.

Embroidery Hoop

When you are working on a canvas that's not very stiff, you will sometimes need an embroidery hoop. This will keep the canvas taut and keep your stitches even.

Fabric

The size of your finished work depends on the fabric you choose. The fewer stitches it has per inch, the larger your cross stitched work of art will measure.

Aida Cloth

Aida cloth is easy to use. The intercrossing of the threads forms even squares, and each square has defined holes in each corner. Aida cloth comes in various sizes, such as 14 count, 16 count, and 18 count. The size indicates the number of holes, or stitches, per inch.

Linen and Other Evenweave Fabrics

Linen is another option. The most common linen fabrics for cross stitch are 28 count or 32 count. Yes, that means linen has about double the number of holes as Aida cloth, but usually when stitching on linen you do not make a cross stitch on every "square" of the fabric. You skip some holes. On 28-count linen, you might skip one hole per stitch. That would equate to working on 14-count Aida cloth.

Evenweave is the term used to describe other fabrics that have an even warp and weft. Typically, evenweave fabrics are smoother than Aida or linen because they contain some man-made fibers.

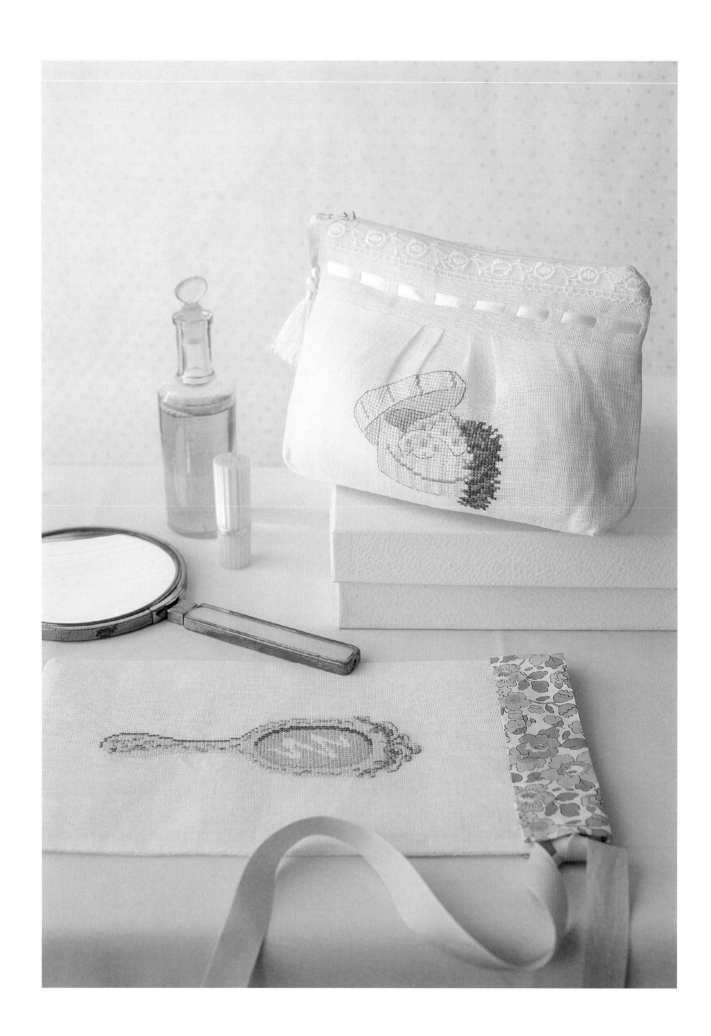

	436		434		801		938
	3841		334		803		834		832

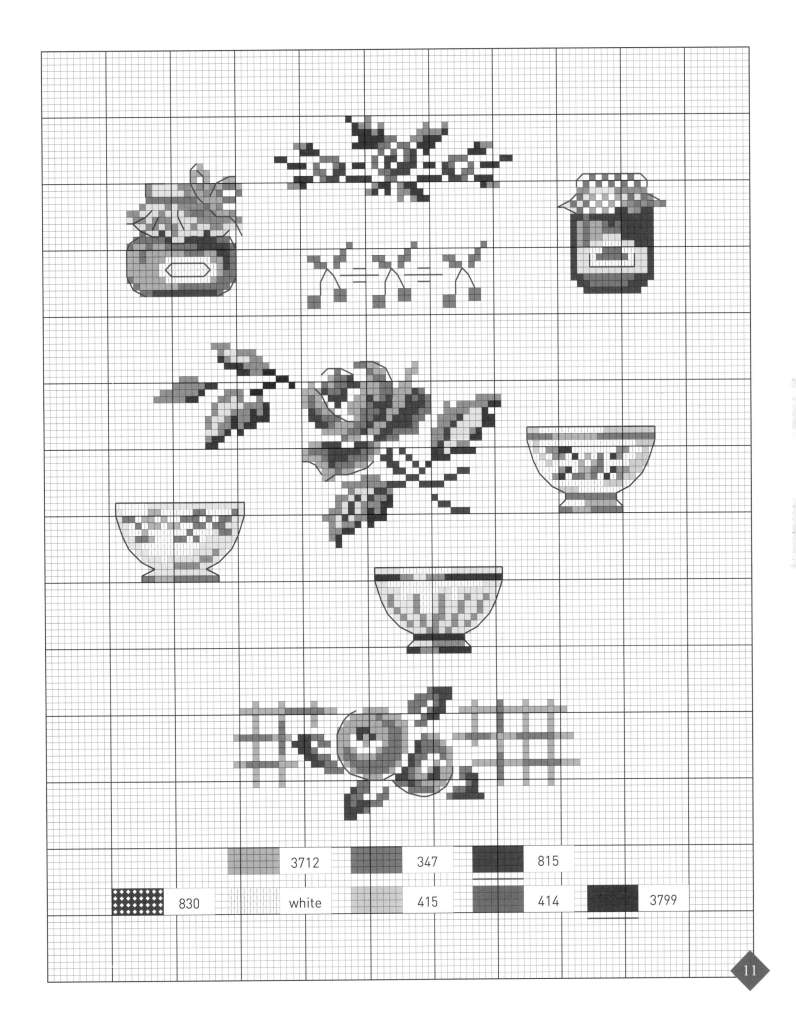

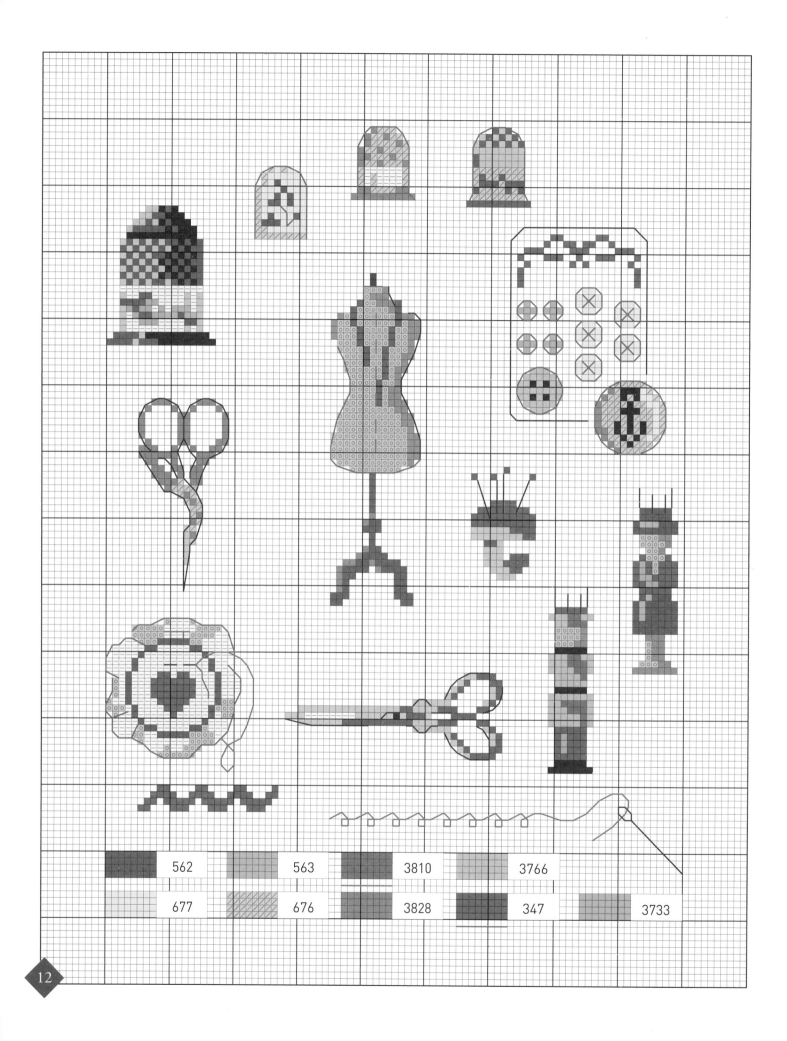

	562		563		3810		3766
	677		676		3828		347		3733

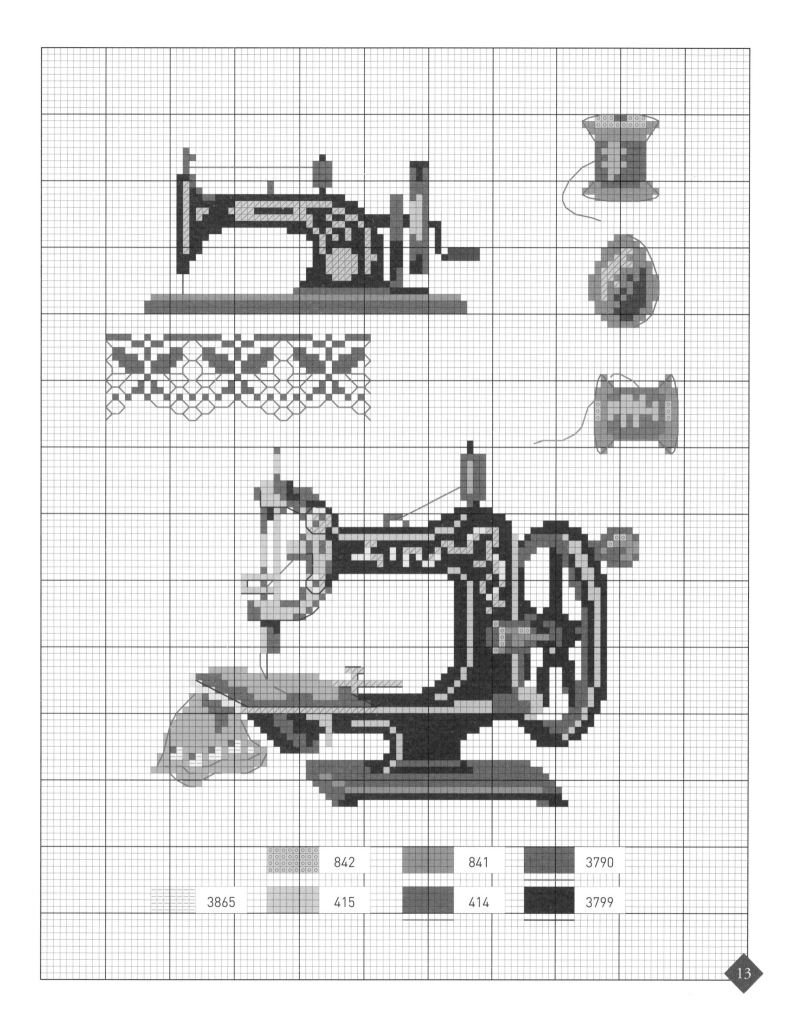

	842		841		3790
	3865		415		414		3799

	341		155		3815		993
	3834		553		3687		605		819

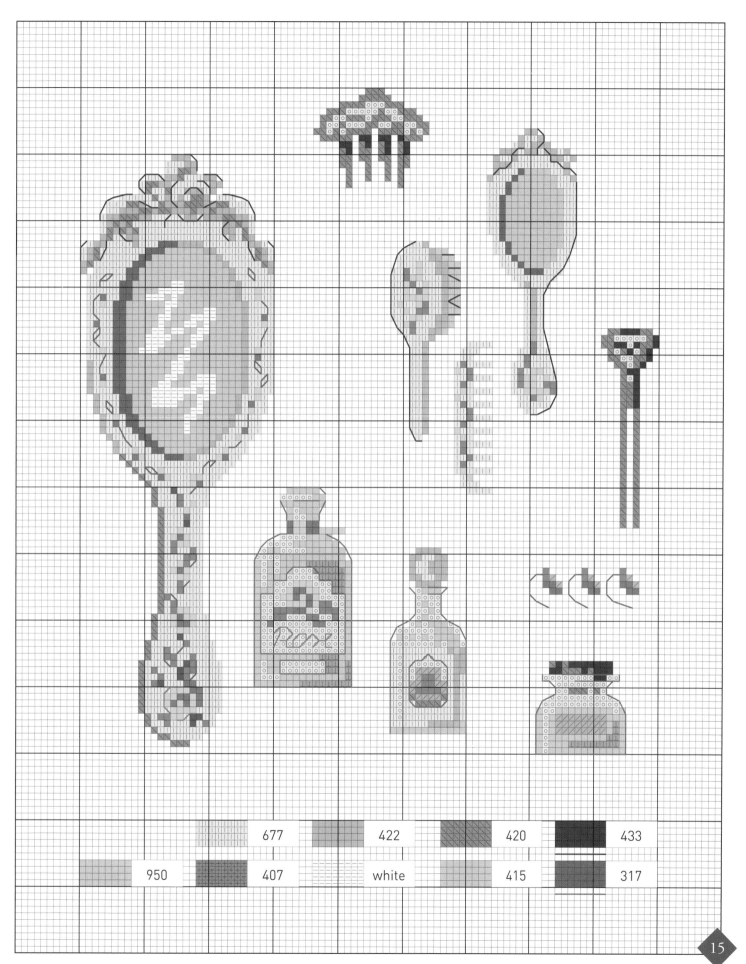

	677		422		420		433
	950		407		white		415		317

A photo of the large mirror is on page 6.

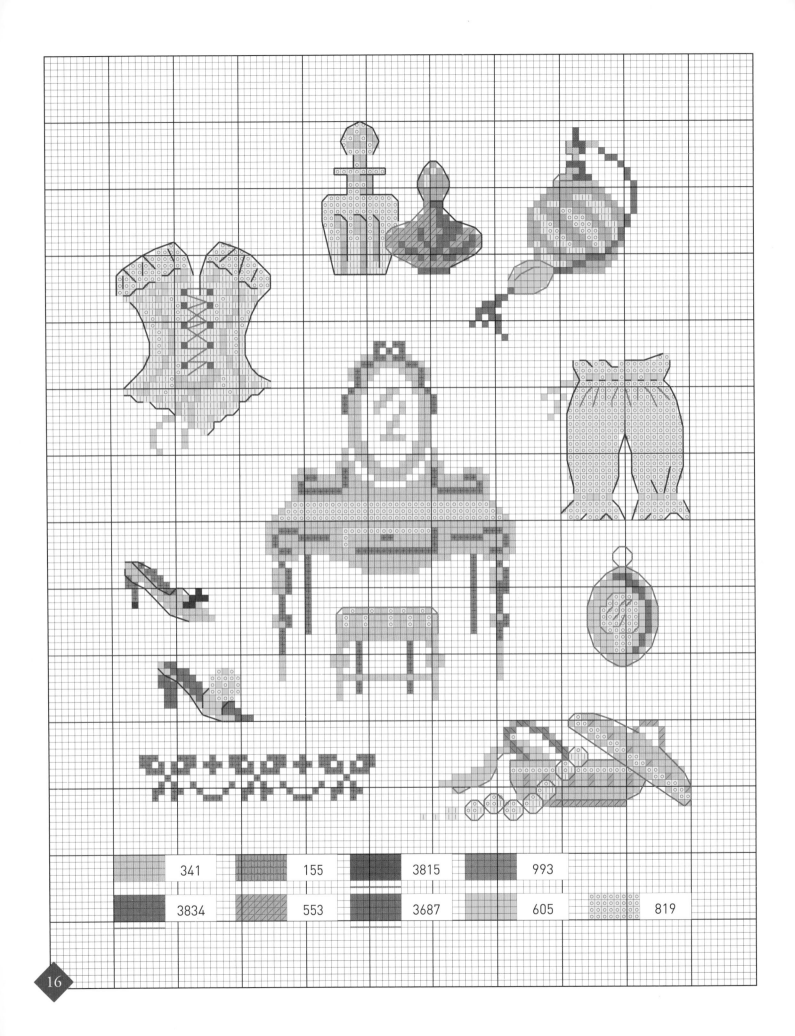

	341		155		3815		993
	3834		553		3687		605		819

	677		422		420		779
	950		407		white		415		317

A photo of the hat box (bottom left) is on page 6.

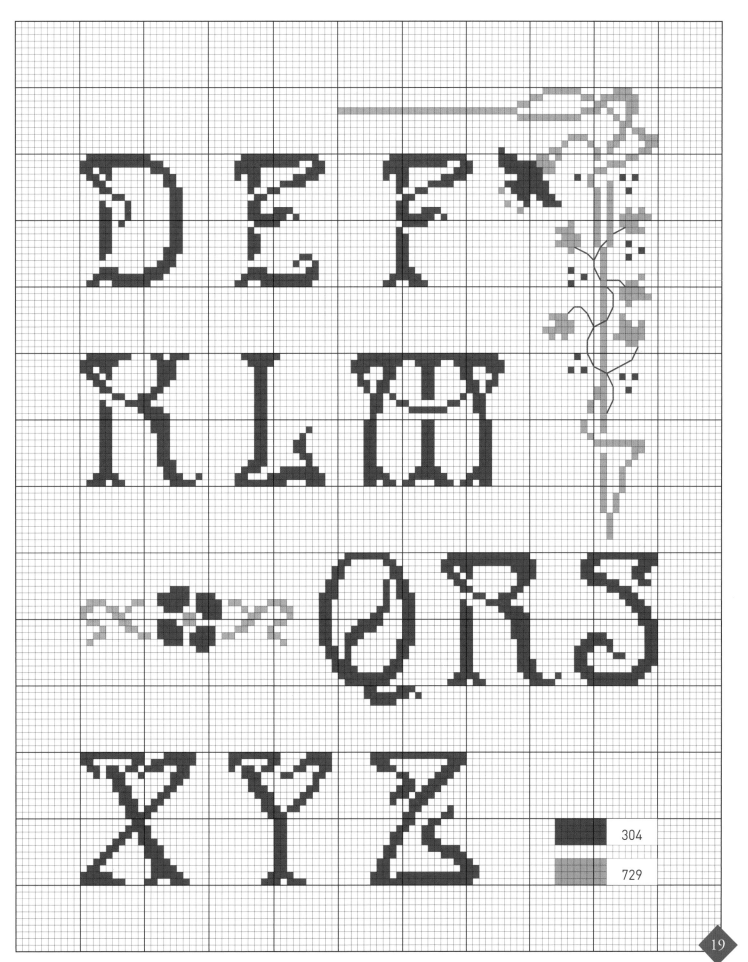

A photo of the letters is on page 8.

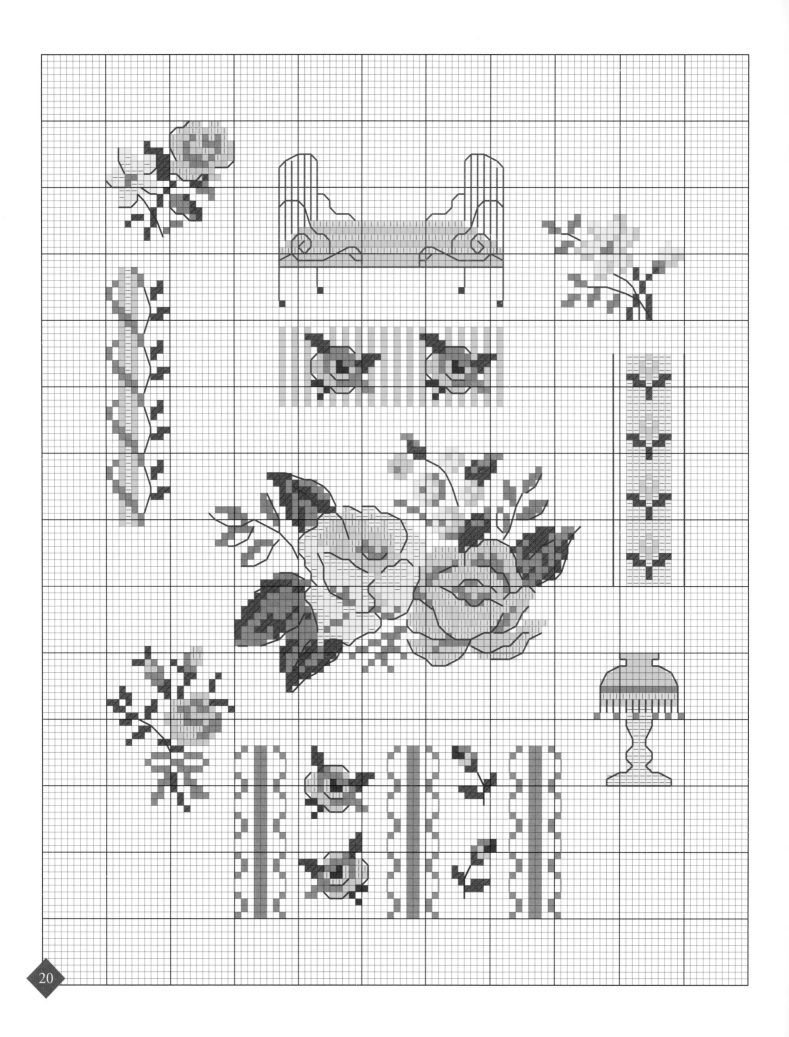

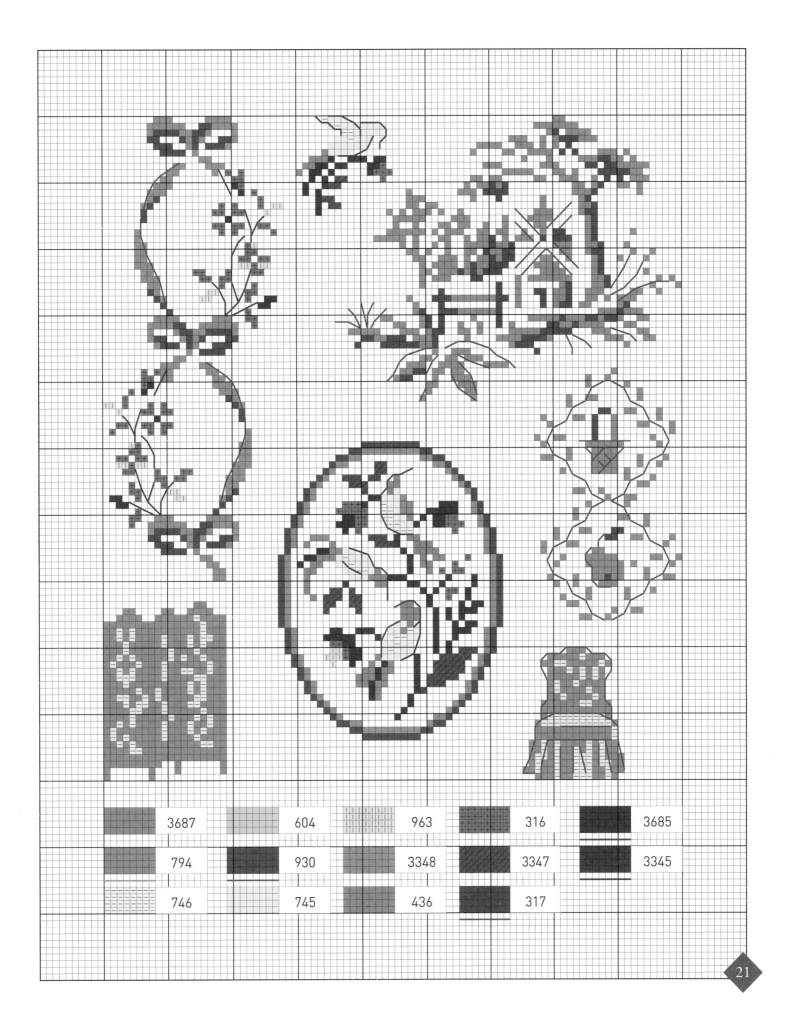

	3687		604		963		316		3685
	794		930		3348		3347		3345
	746		745		436		317		

	948		754		3831		777		3837
	368		987		677		977		436

A photo of the little boy is on page 7.
A photo of the street sign is on page 7.

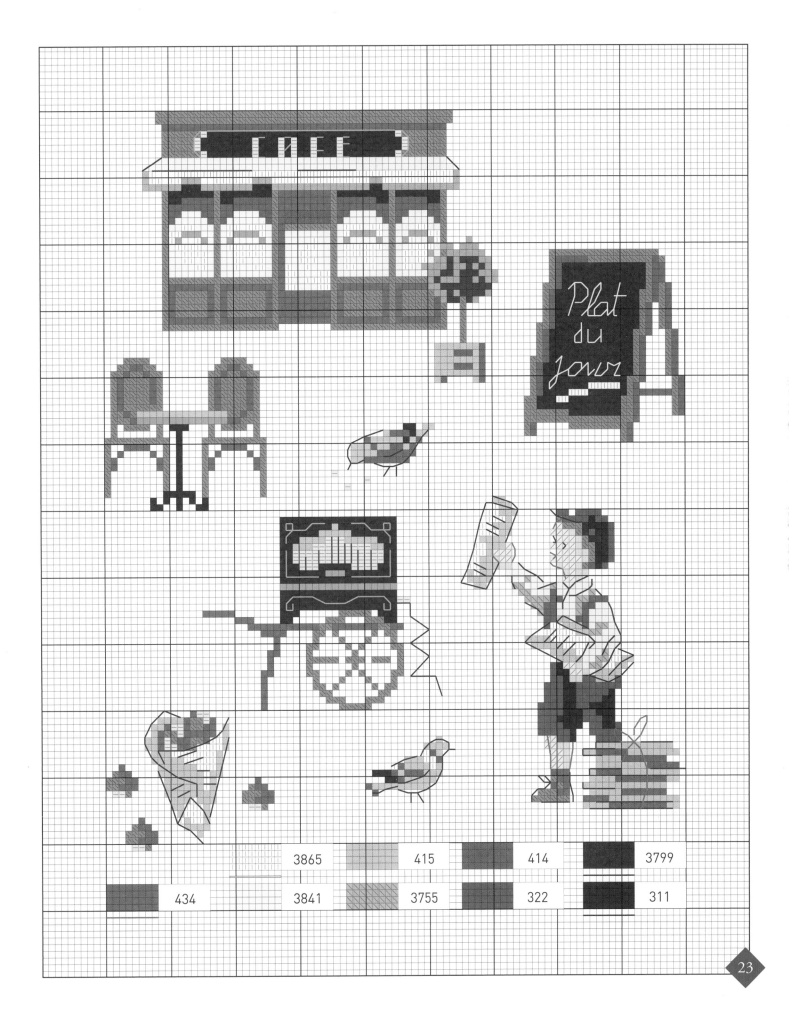

	3865		415		414		3799
	434		3841		3755		322		311

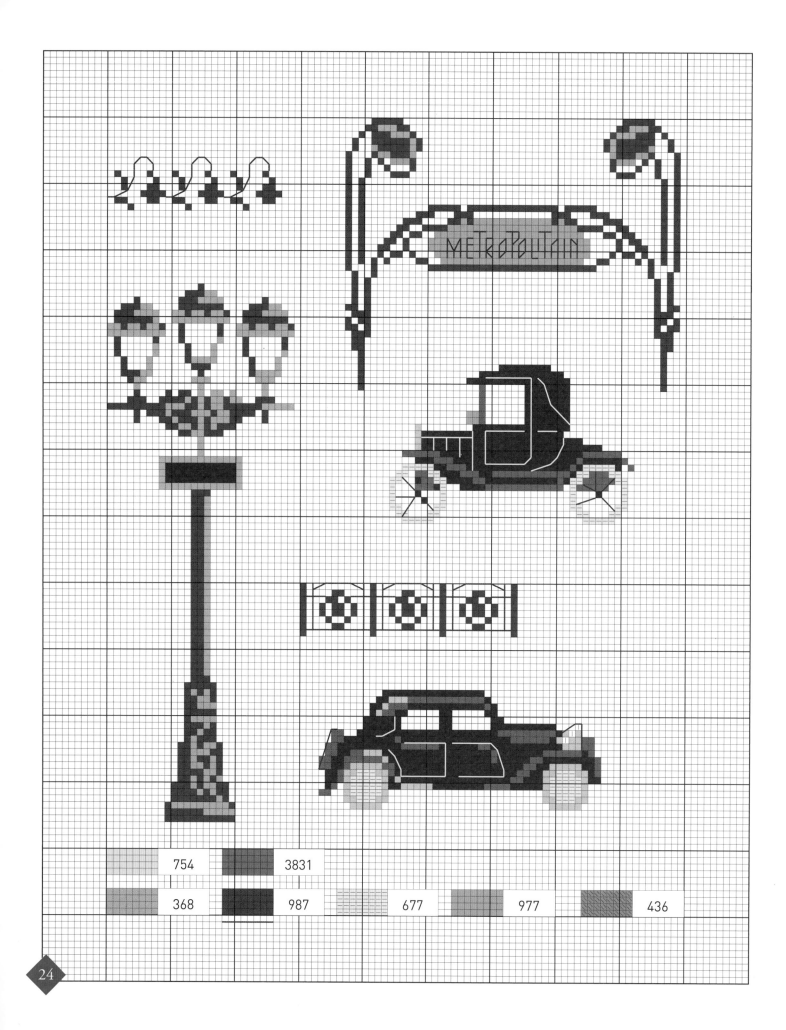

	754		3831
	368		987		677		977		436

24

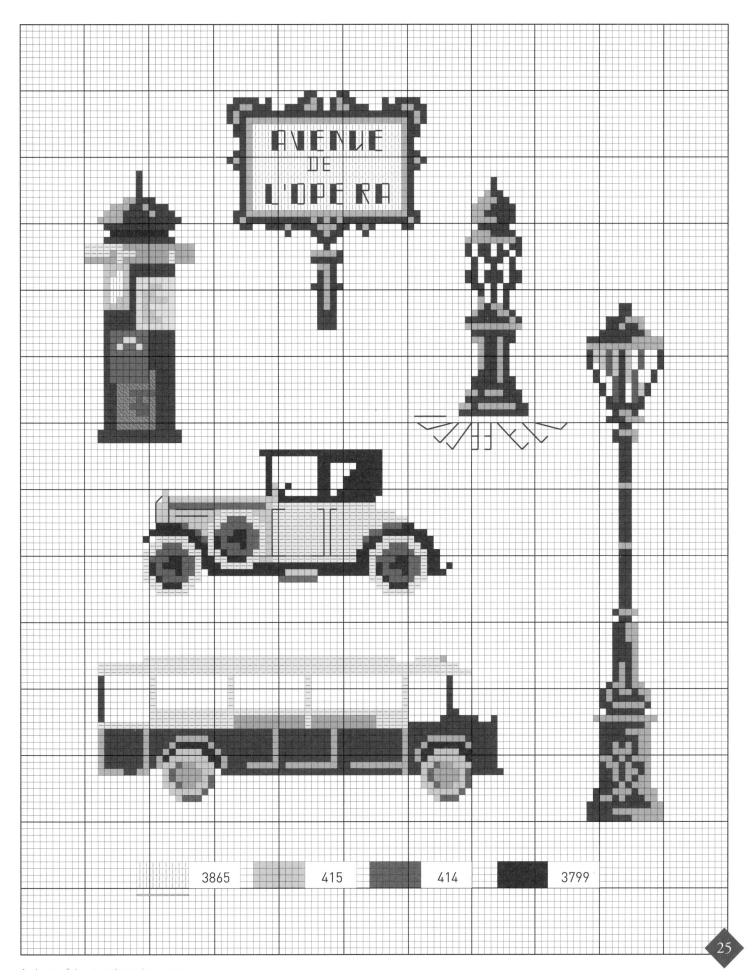

AVENUE DE L'OPERA

| | 3865 | | 415 | | 414 | | 3799 |

A photo of the streetlamp is on page 7.

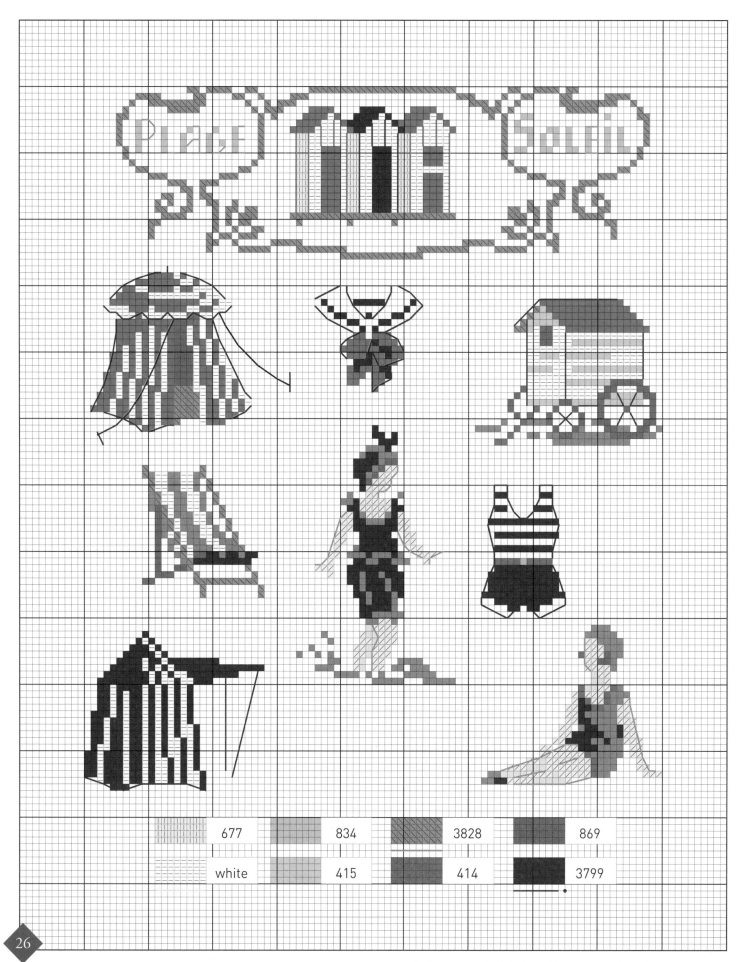

677   834   3828   869

white   415   414   3799

A photo of the deckchair, the blue tent, and the cabana is on page 9.

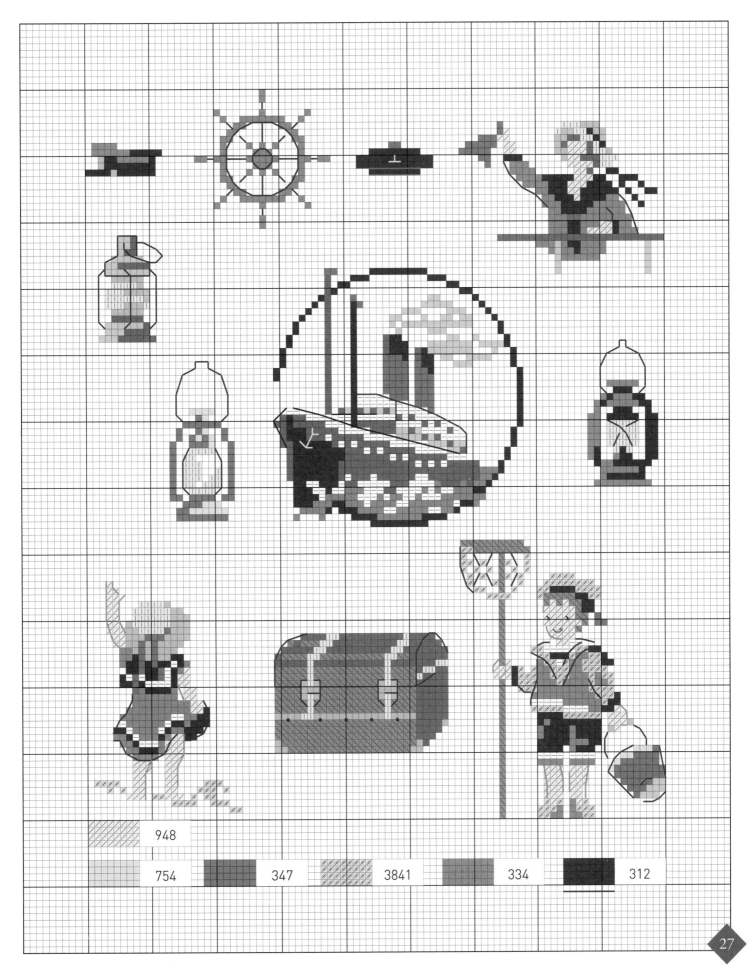

	948										
	754		347		3841		334		312

A photo of the top right design is on page 9.

Pasteur
Curie
Niepce
Daguerre
Lumière
Remmyton
Edison
Bell
Marconi

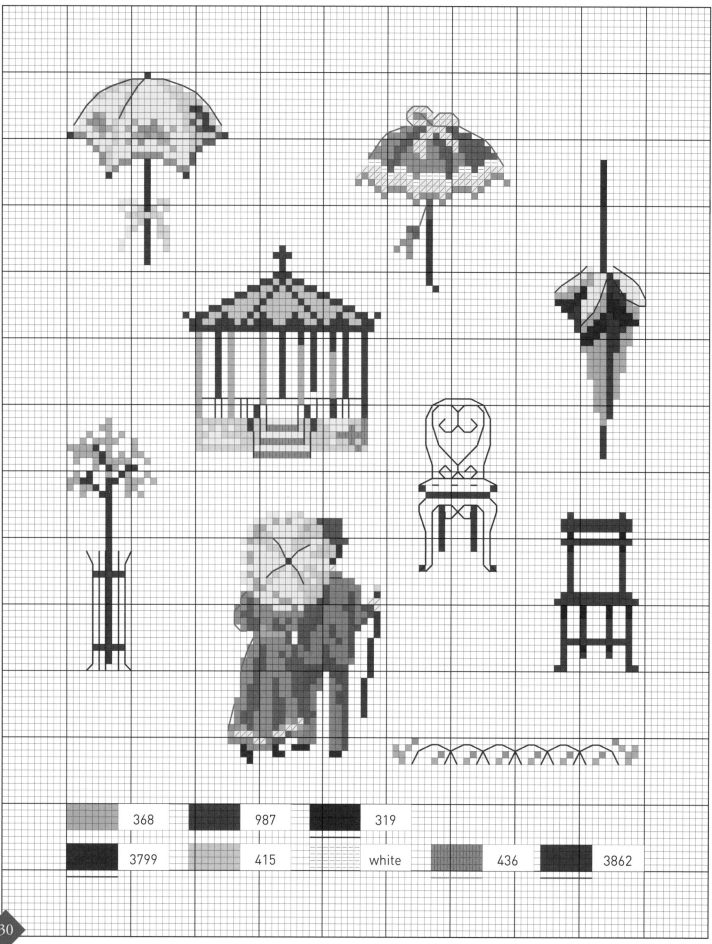

	368		987		319
	3799		415		white

	436		3862

	3325		322		3750		948
	604		3731		3803		677		676

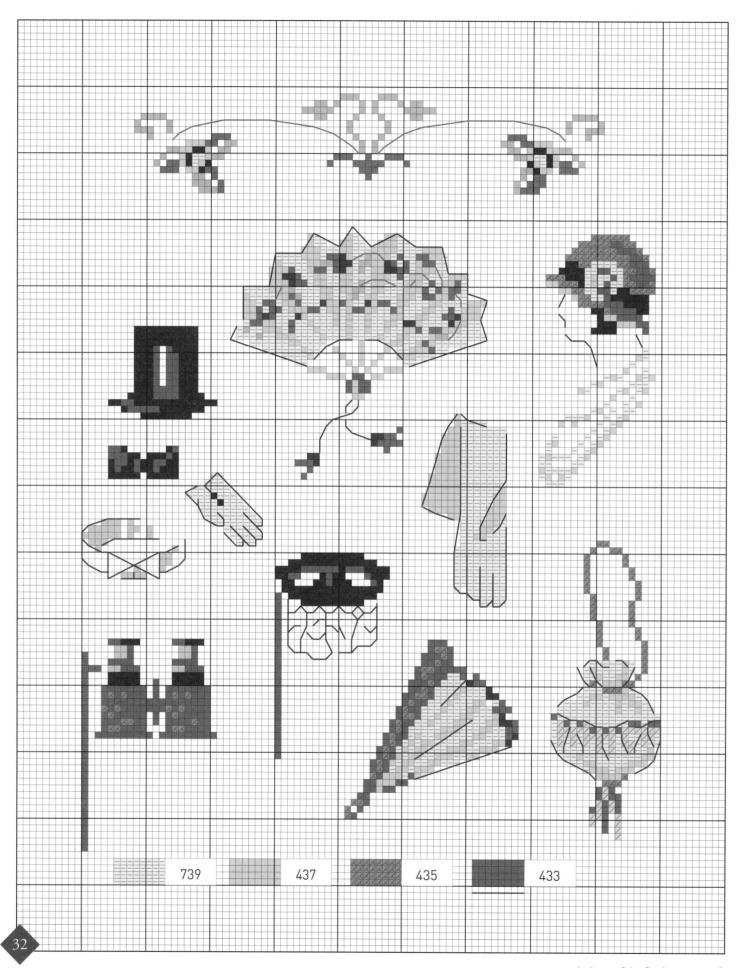

| | 739 | | 437 | | 435 | | 433 |

A photo of the fan is on page 28.

	347		815		519		517
	415		414		3799		3821

33

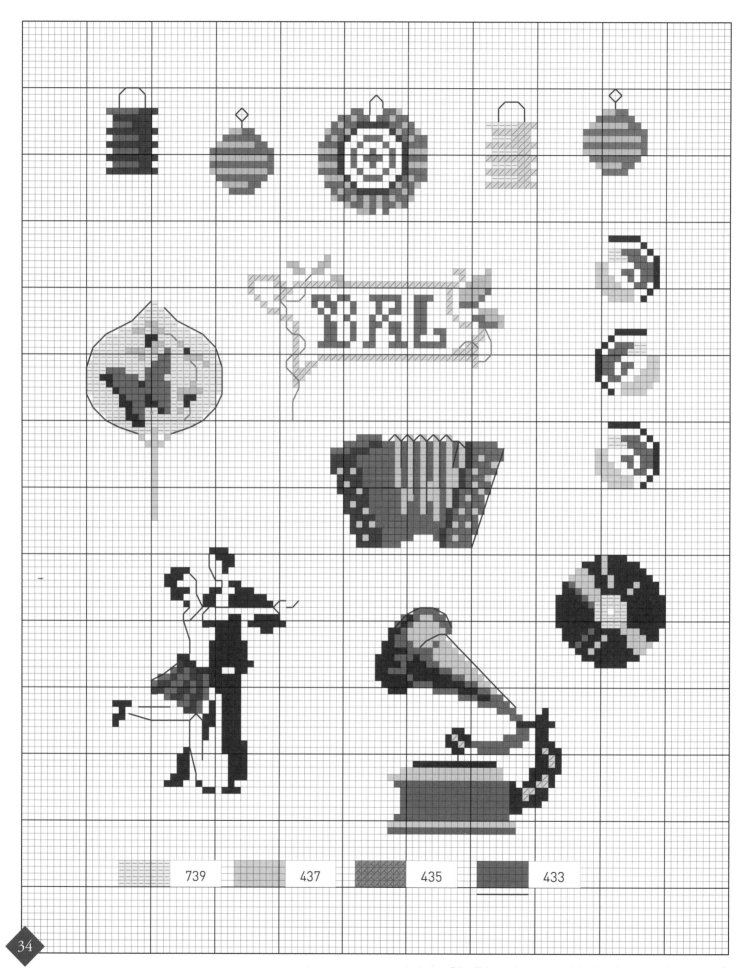

	739		437		435		433

A photo of the Chinese lanterns and the dancing couple is on page 28.

	347		815		519		517
	415		414		3799		3821

A photo of the dancer is on page 28.

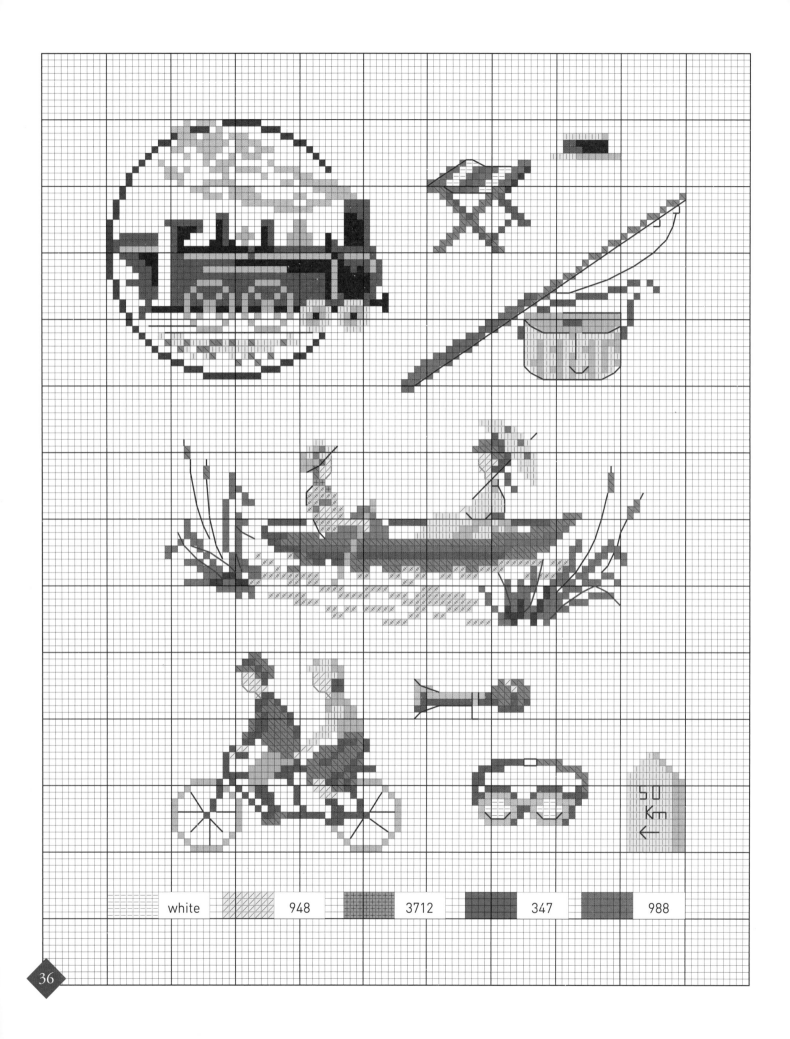

| | white | | 948 | | 3712 | | 347 | | 988 |

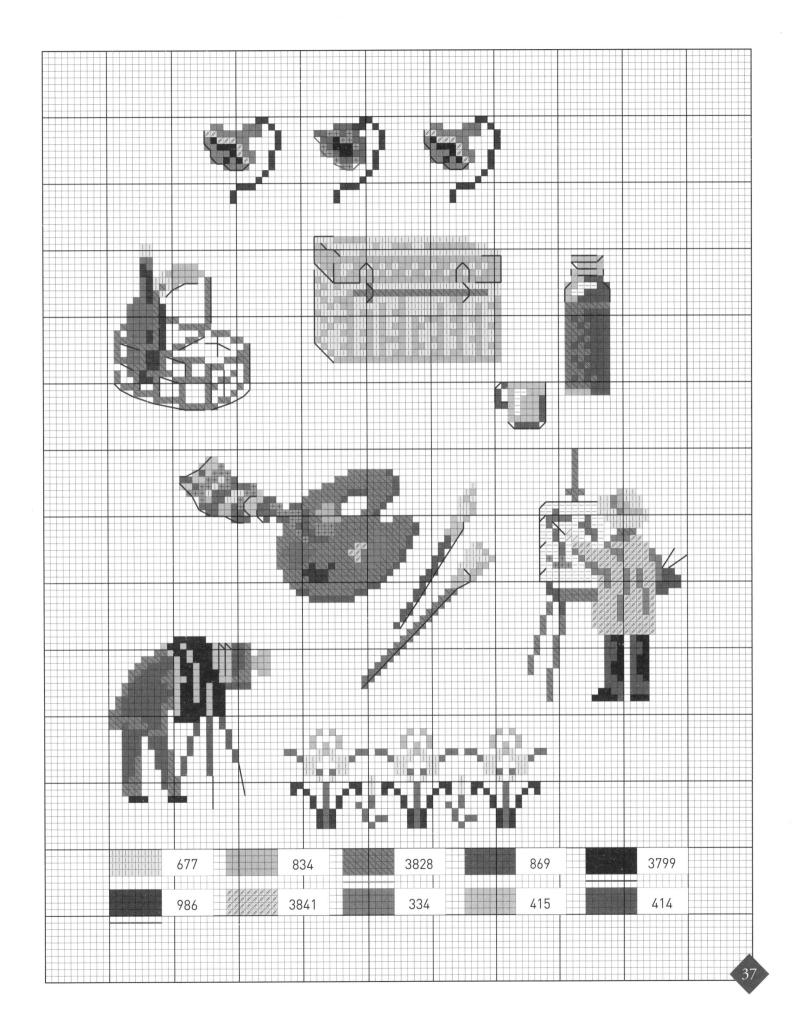

	677		834		3828		869		3799
	986		3841		334		415		414

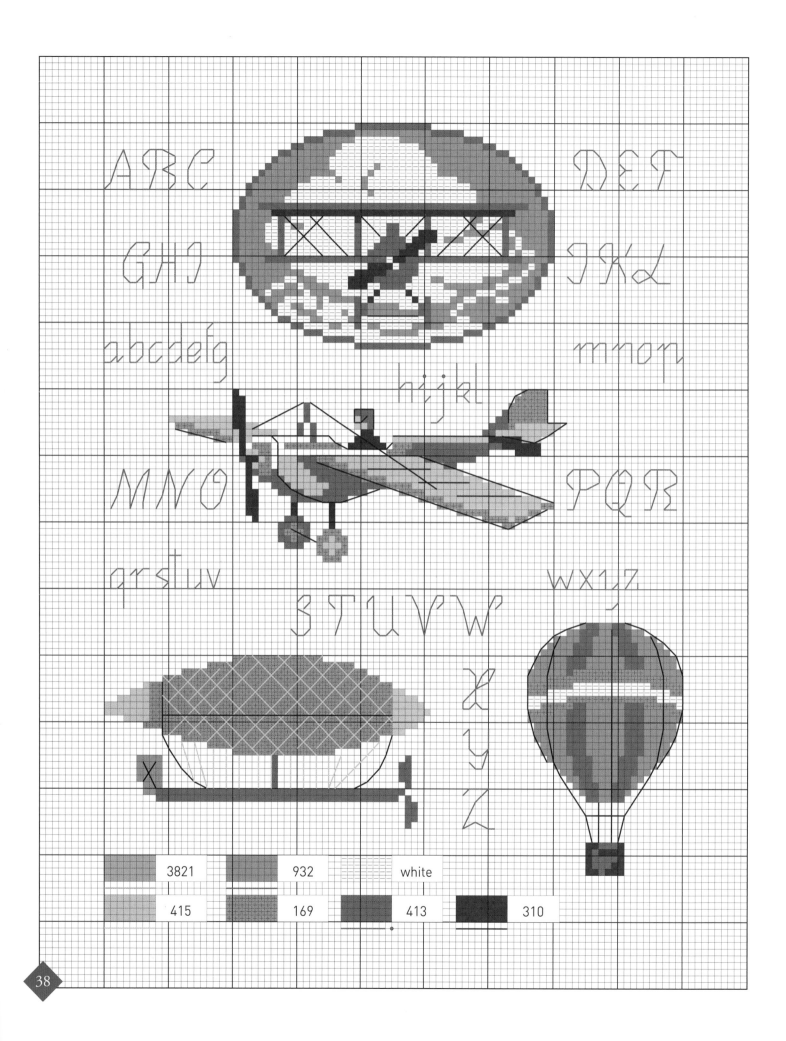

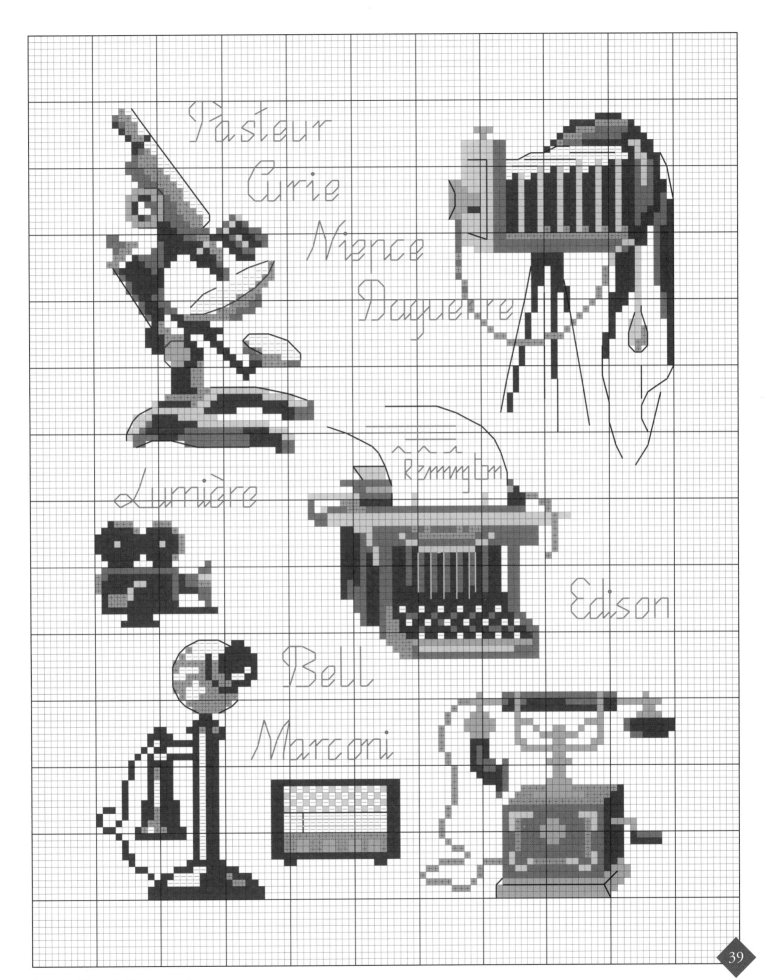

Pasteur
Curie
Niepce
Daguerre
Lumière
Remington
Edison
Bell
Marconi

A photo of these designs is on page 29.

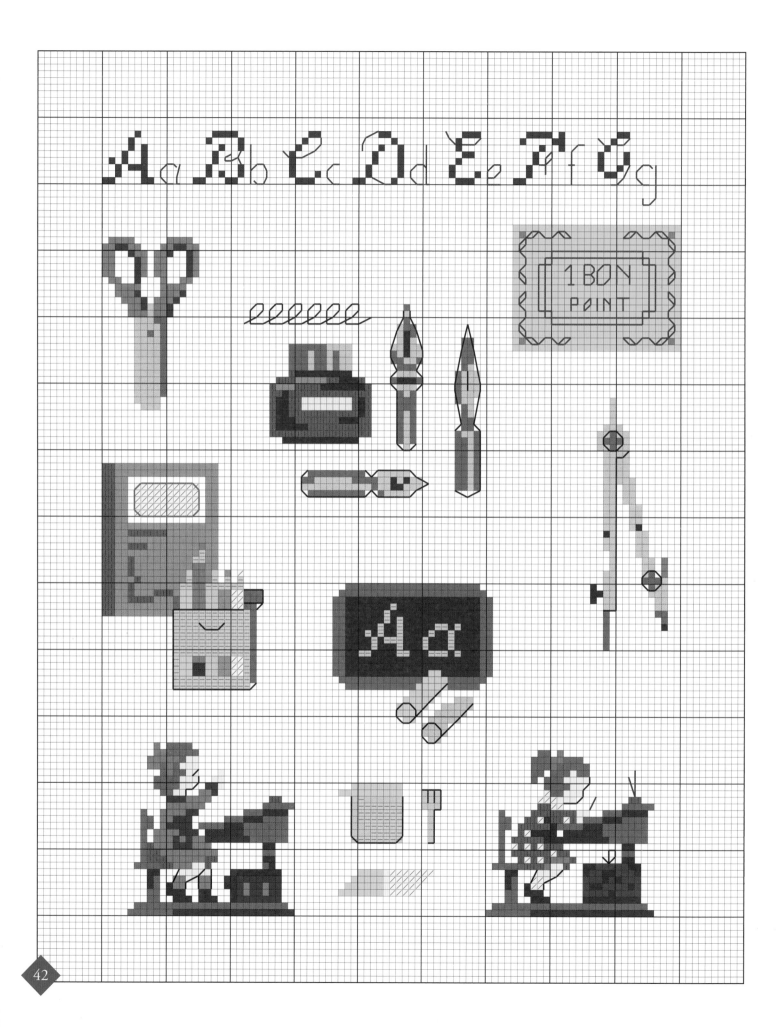

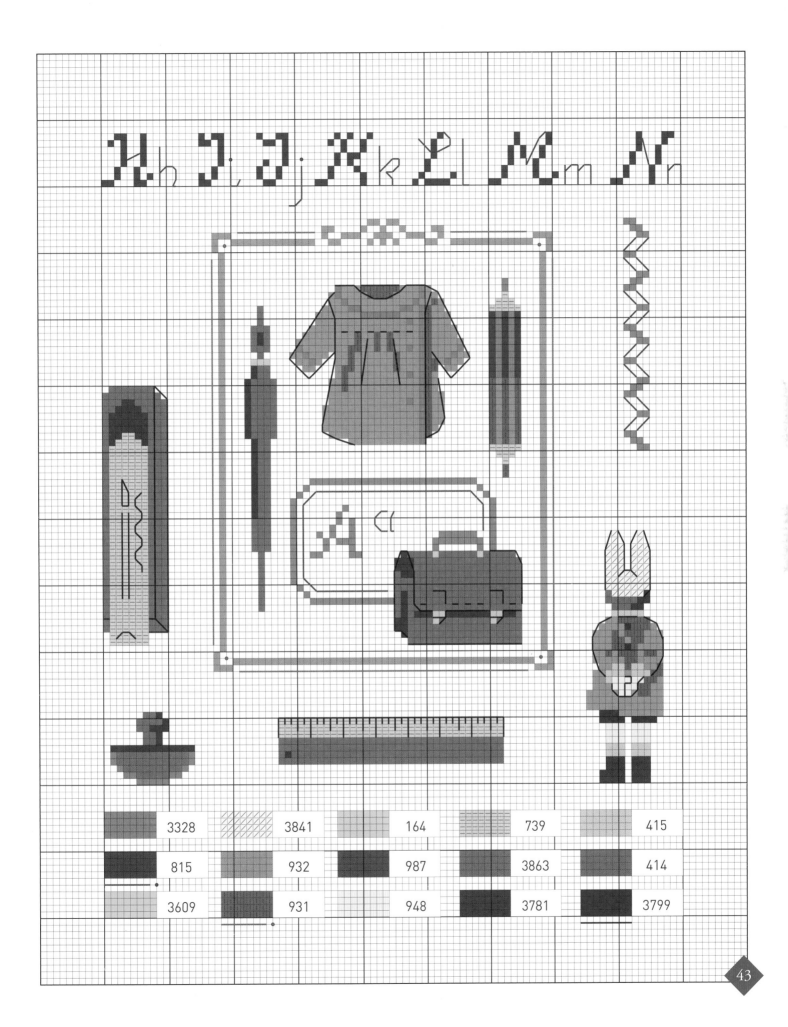

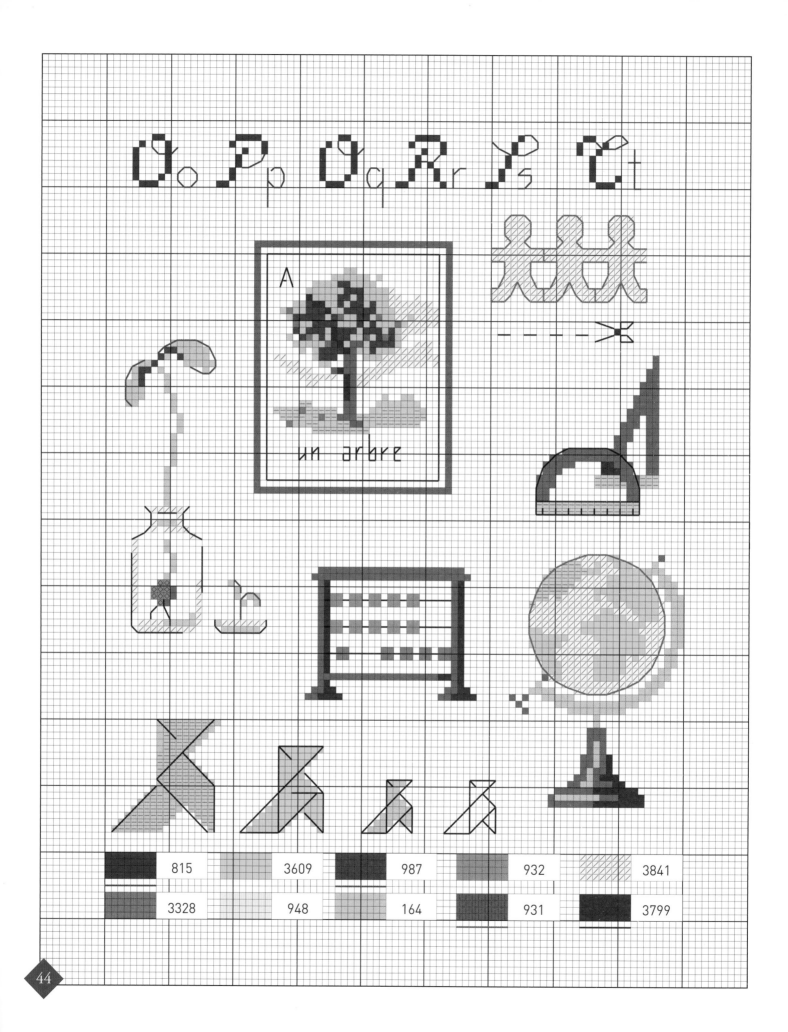

un arbre

	815		3609		987		932		3841
	3328		948		164		931		3799

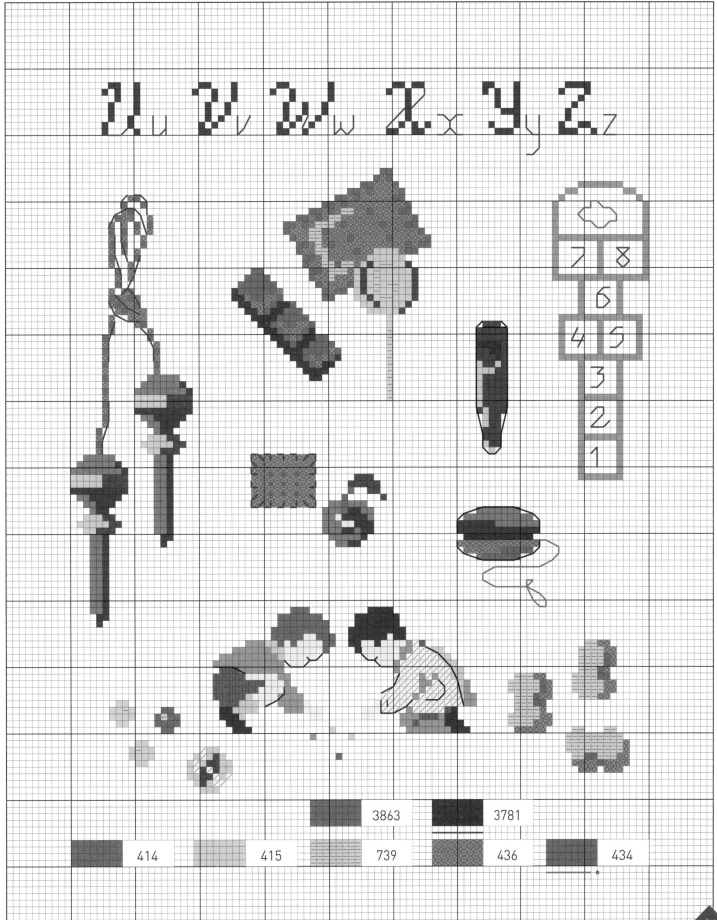

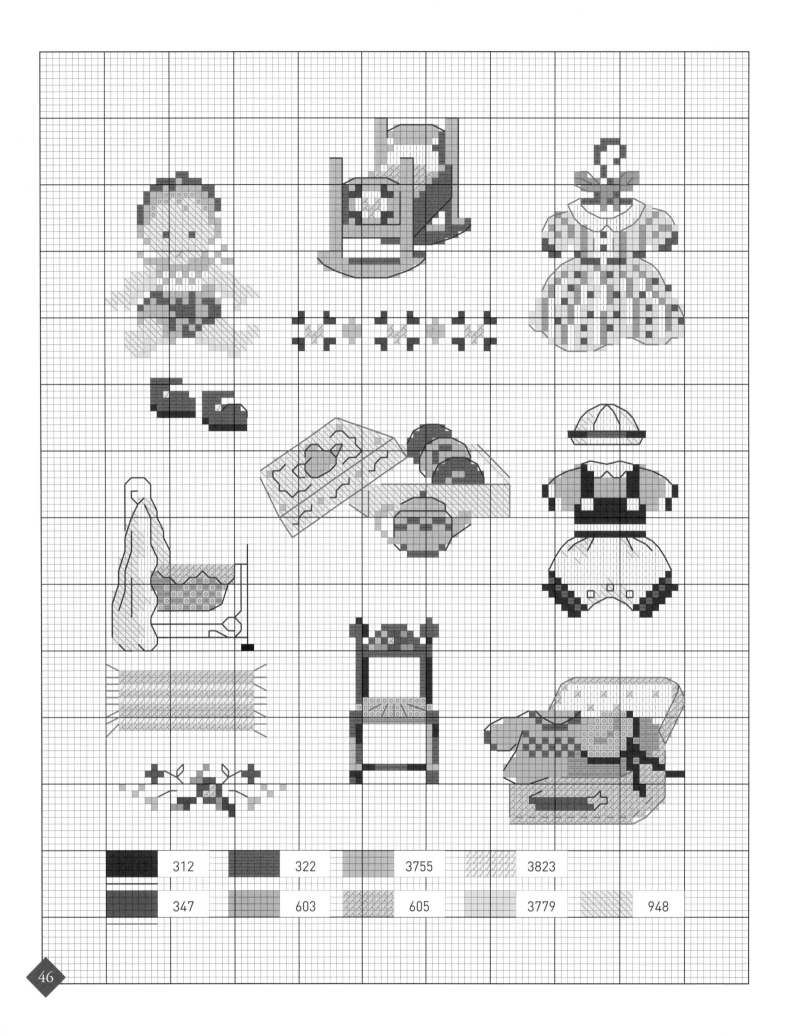

	986		988		white
	676		729		435		433		3371

A photo of the top right design is on page 41.

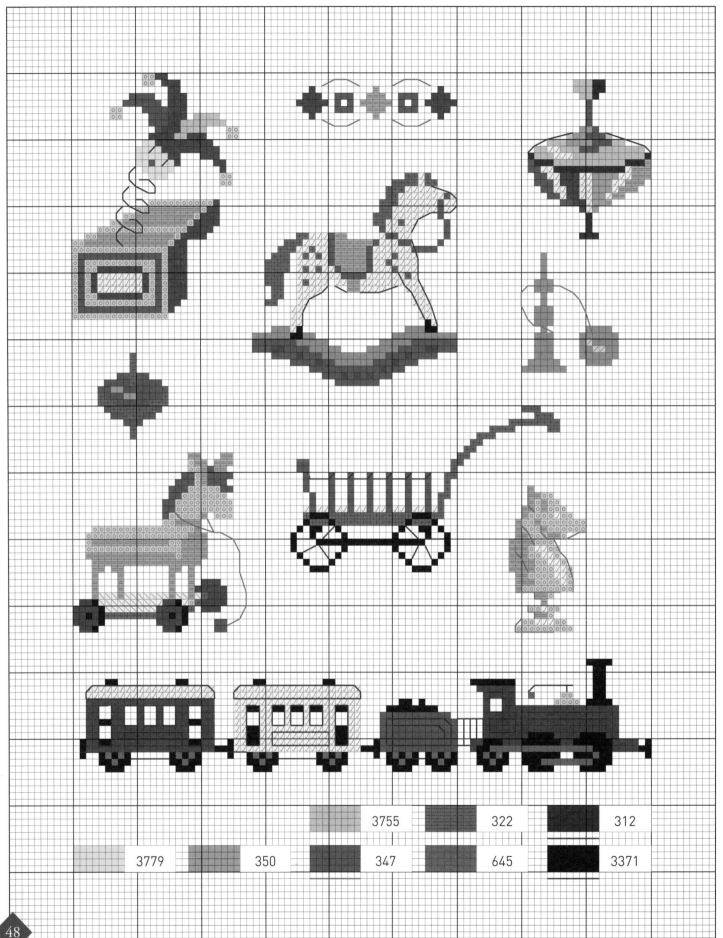

	3755		322		312
	3779		350		347		645		3371

A photo of the bottom design is on page 41.

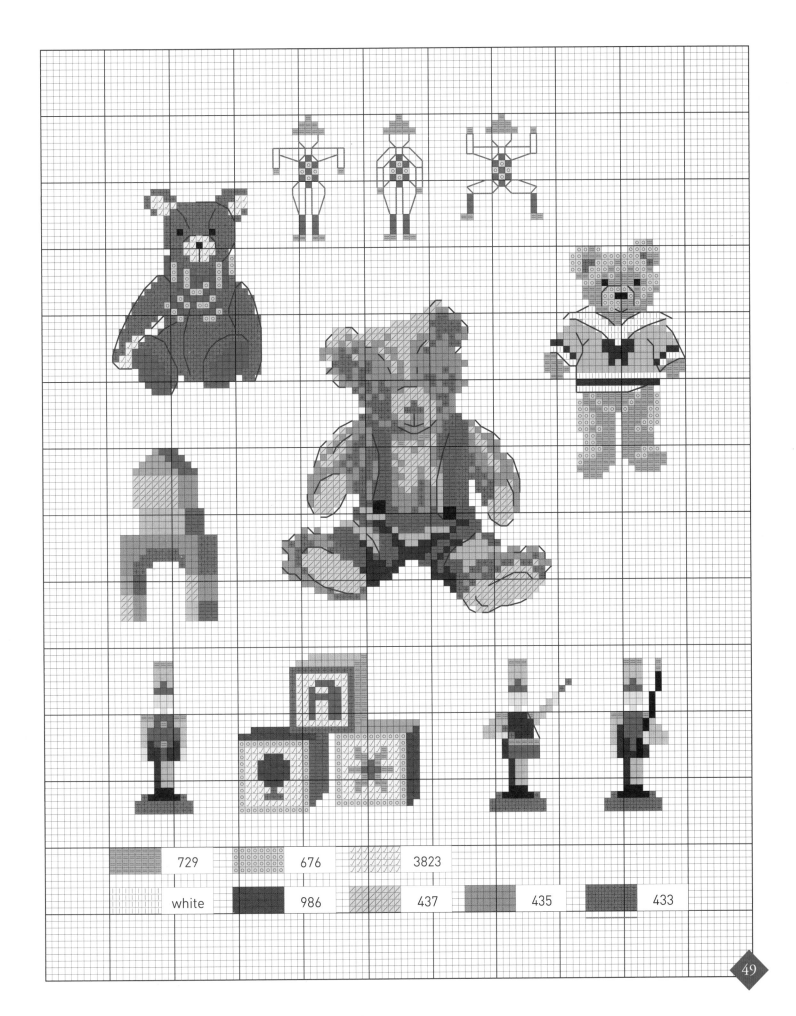

| 729 | 676 | 3823 |
| white | 986 | 437 | 435 | 433 |

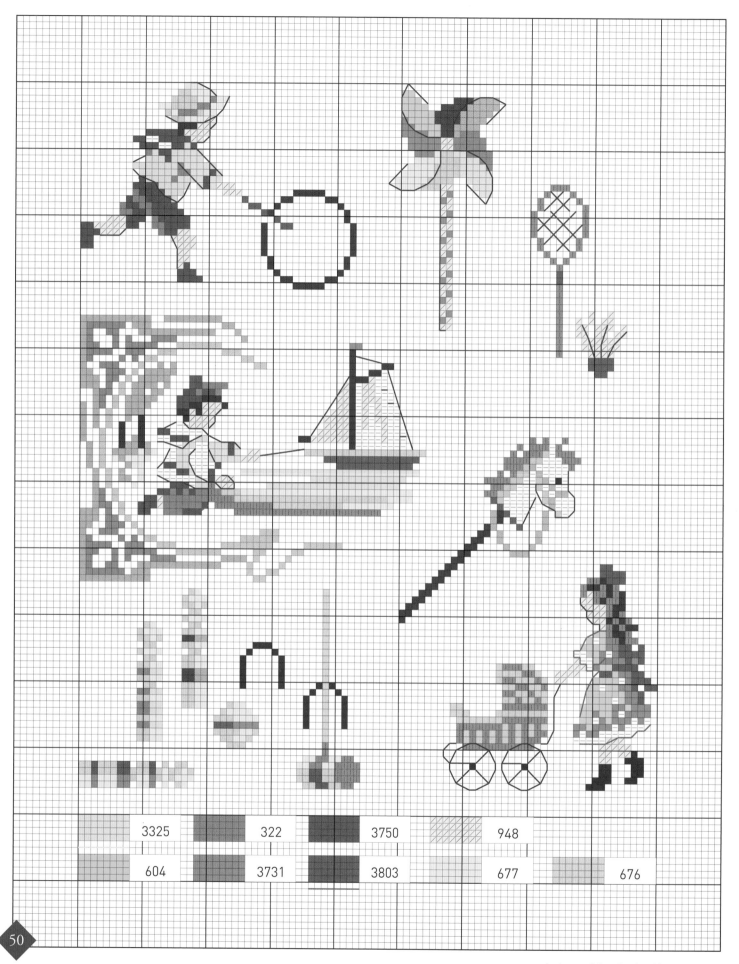

	3325		322		3750		948
	604		3731		3803		677		676

A photo of the pinwheel is on page 40.

	368		987					
	3799		415		white		436		3862

A photo of the gendarme (policeman) puppet is on page 40.

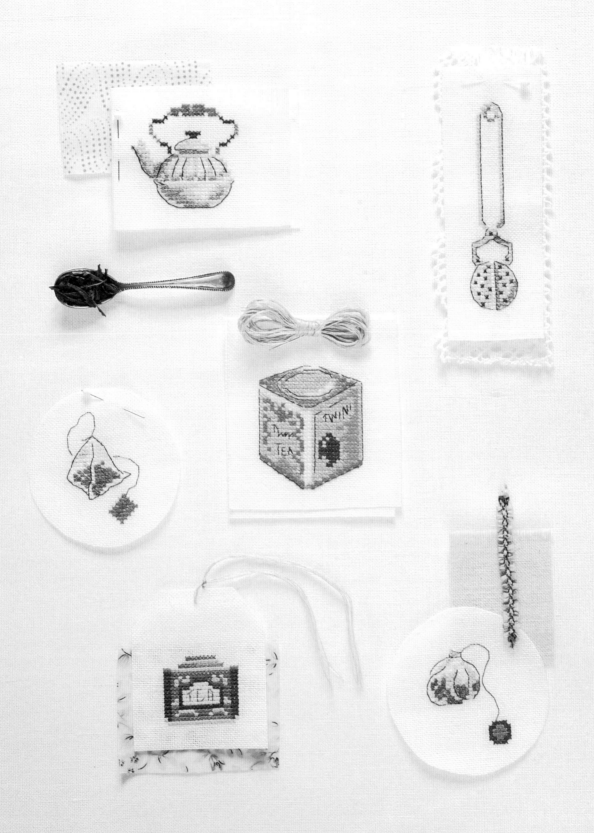

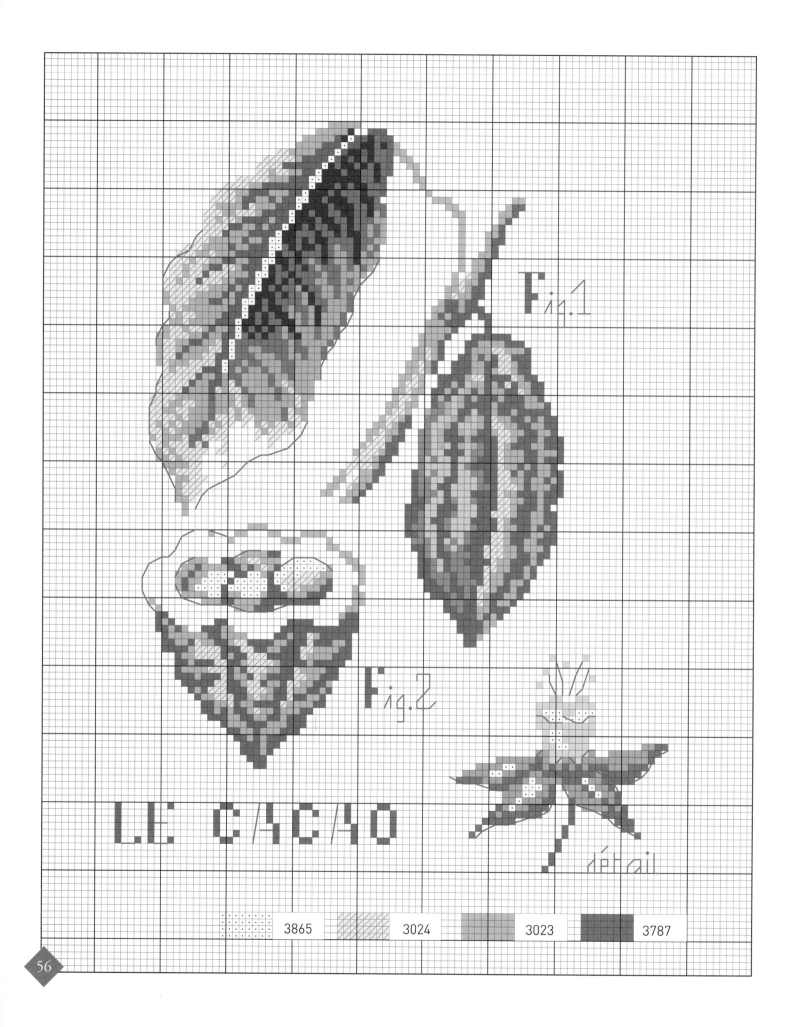

Fig.1

Fig.2

LE CACAO

détail

| | 3865 | | 3024 | | 3023 | | 3787 |

56

Fig. 2

Fig. 3

LE THÉ

Fig. 1

| | 3348 |
| | 3052 |

A photo of these designs is on page 54.

Darjeeling

Ceylon

Oolong   Orange Pekoe

Lapsang   Yunnan
Souchong

        Assam

Matcha   fumé

          blanc
              vert

Earl Grey

| | 3362 | | 3023 | | 3865 | | 3820 | | 3721 |
| | 3787 | | 3024 | | 3822 | | 782 | | 3810 |

59

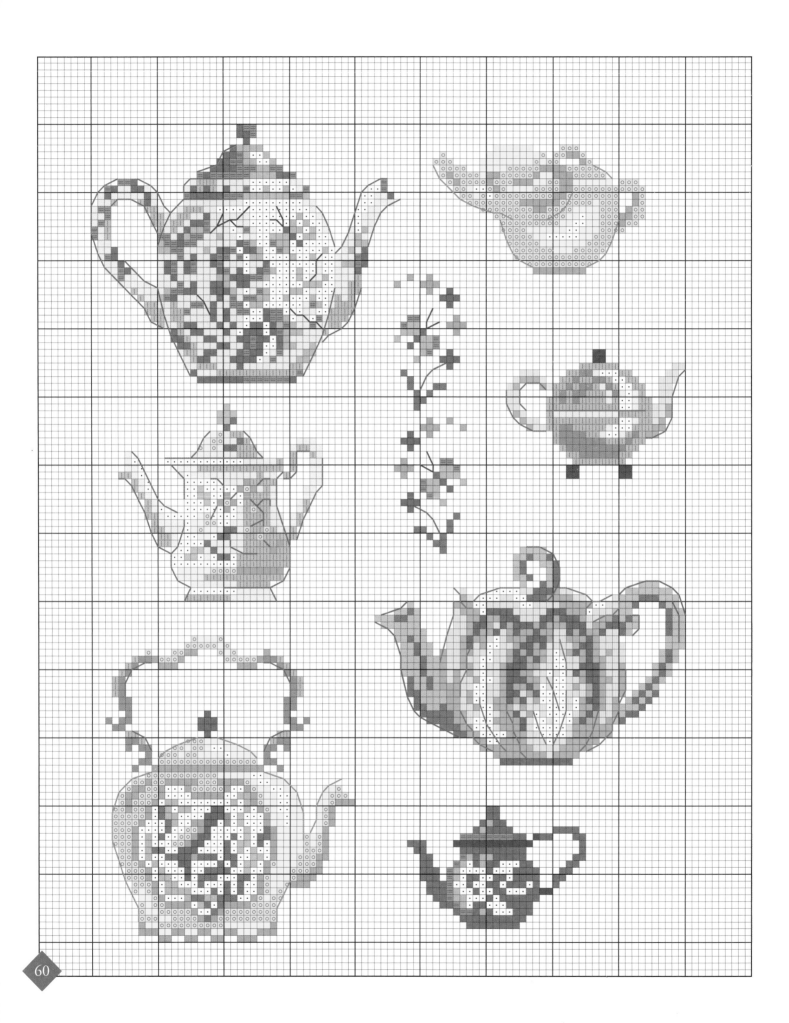

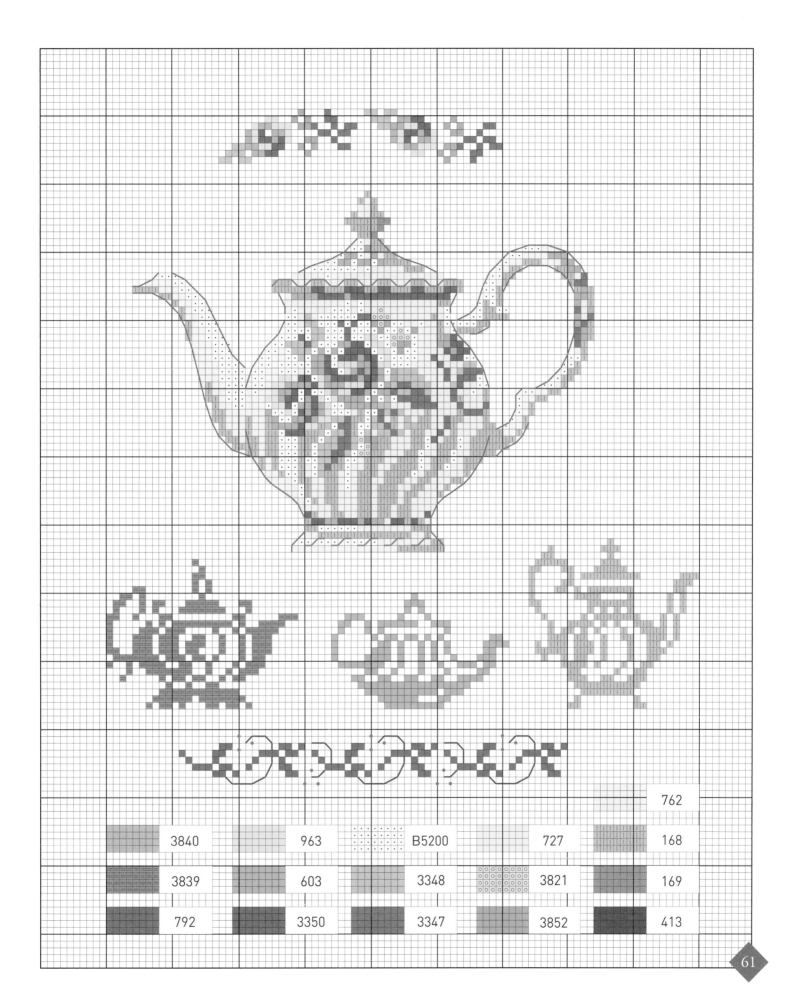

	3840		963		B5200		727		168
										762
	3839		603		3348		3821		169
	792		3350		3347		3852		413

A photo of the center right design is on page 55.

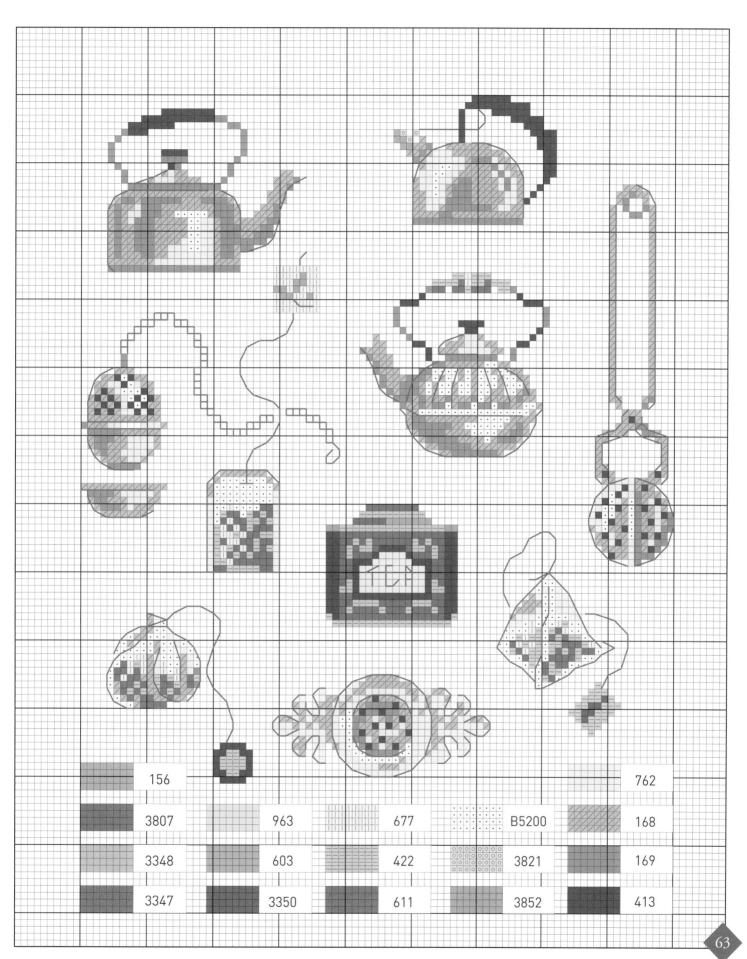

	156								762
	3807		963		677		B5200		168
	3348		603		422		3821		169
	3347		3350		611		3852		413

A photo of these designs is on page 53.

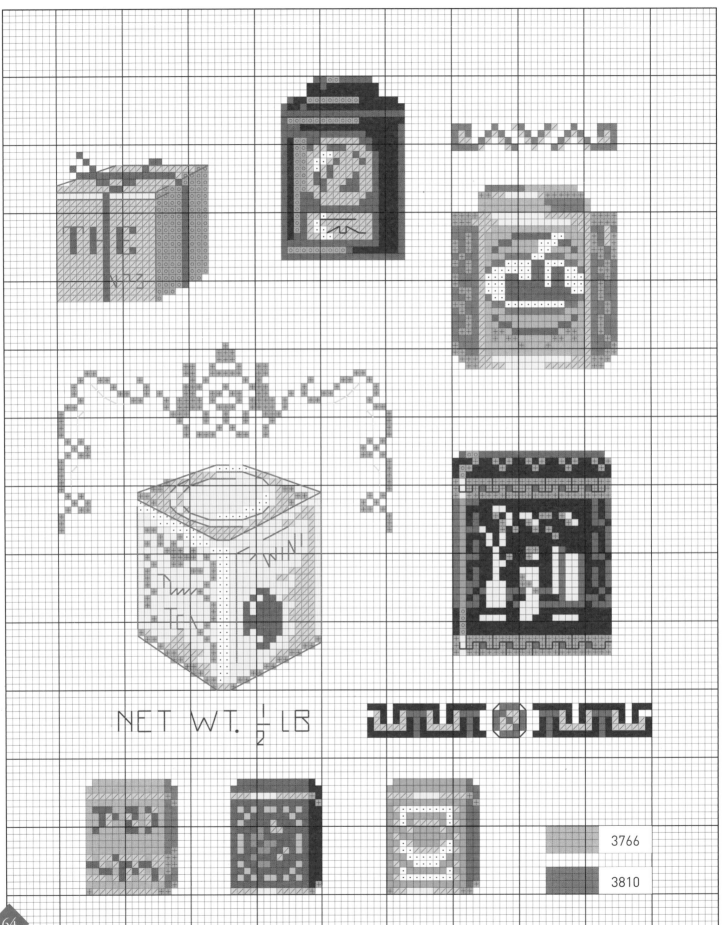

NET WT. ½ LB

3766

3810

A photo of the center design is on page 53.

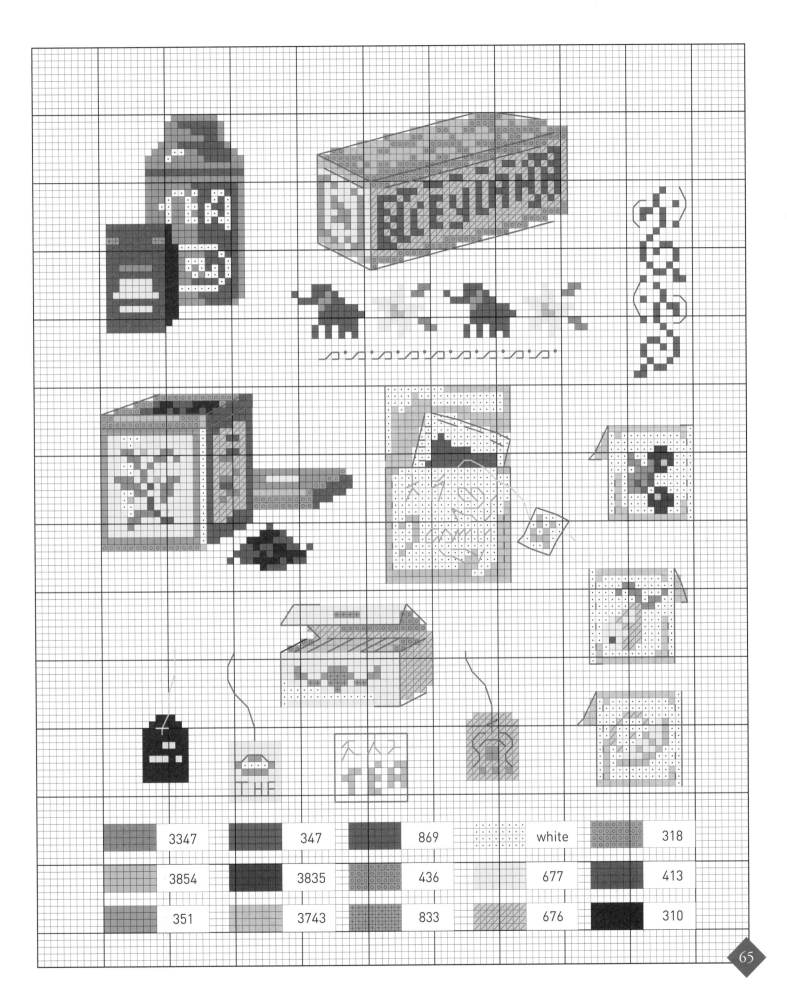

	3347		347		869		white		318
	3854		3835		436		677		413
	351		3743		833		676		310

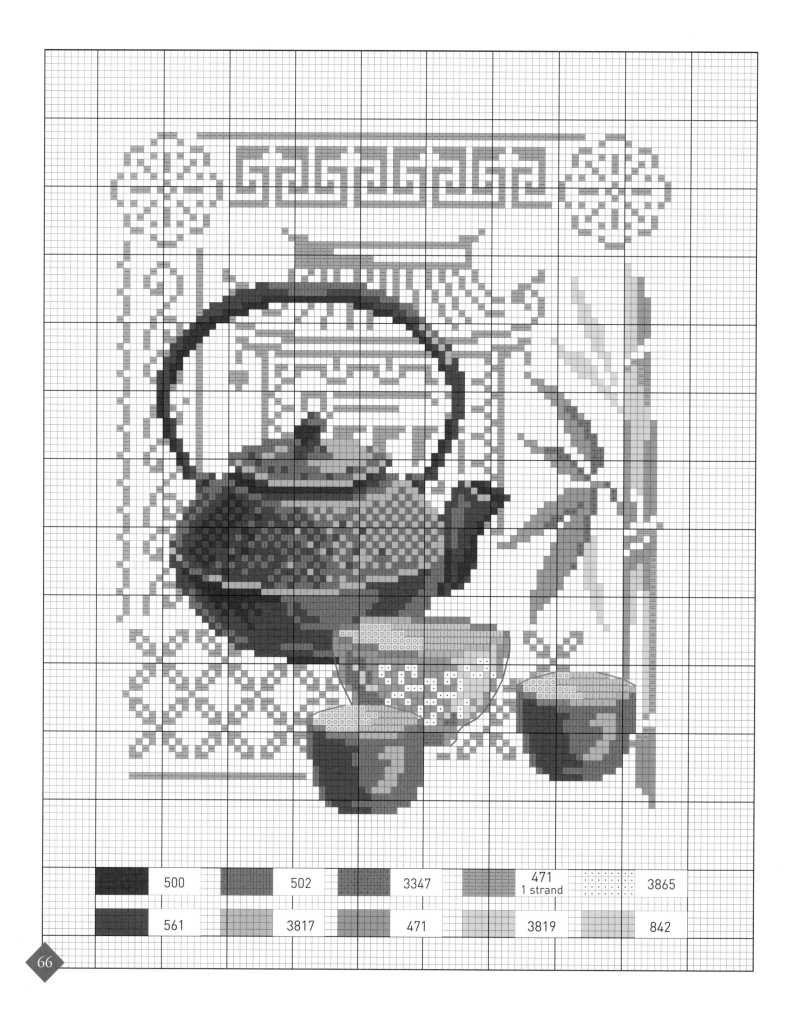

	500		502		3347		471 1 strand		3865
	561		3817		471		3819		842

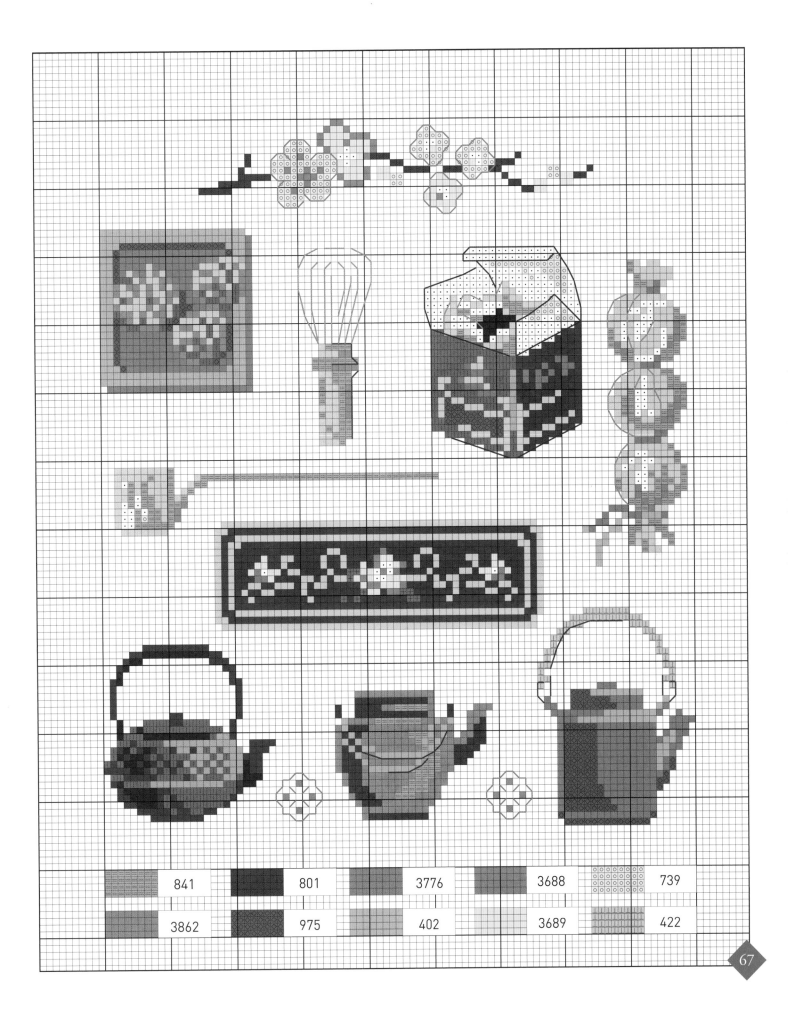

	841		801		3776		3688		739
	3862		975		402		3689		422

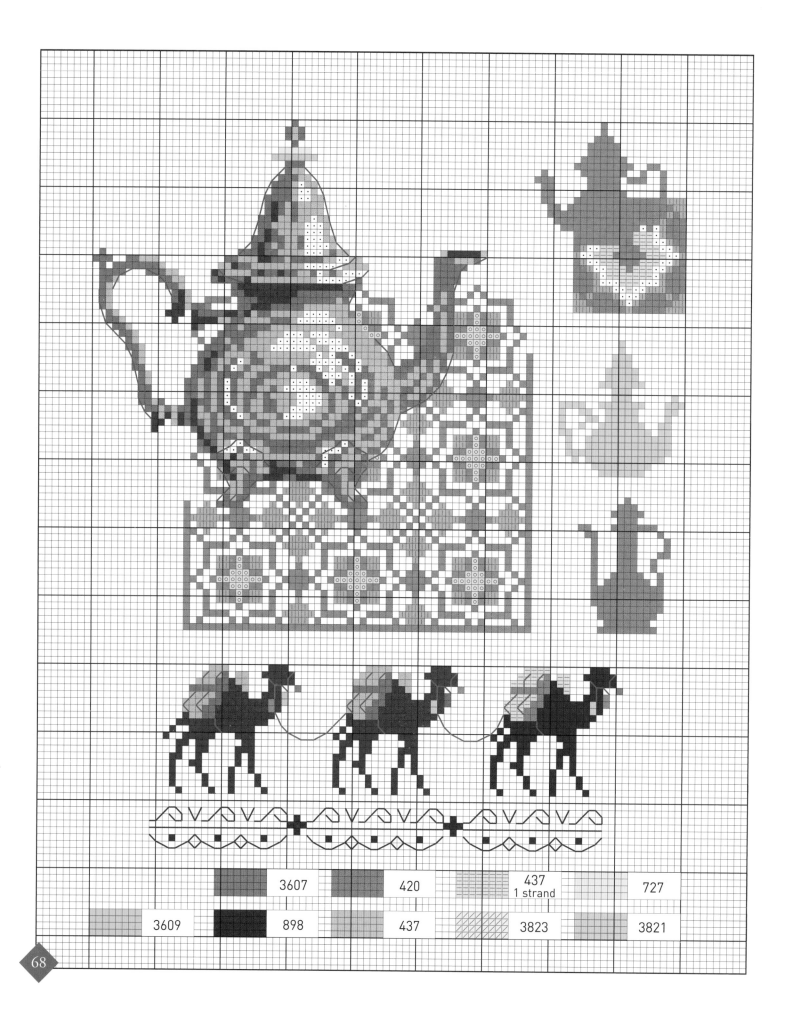

	3607		420		437 1 strand		727
	3609		898		437		3823		3821

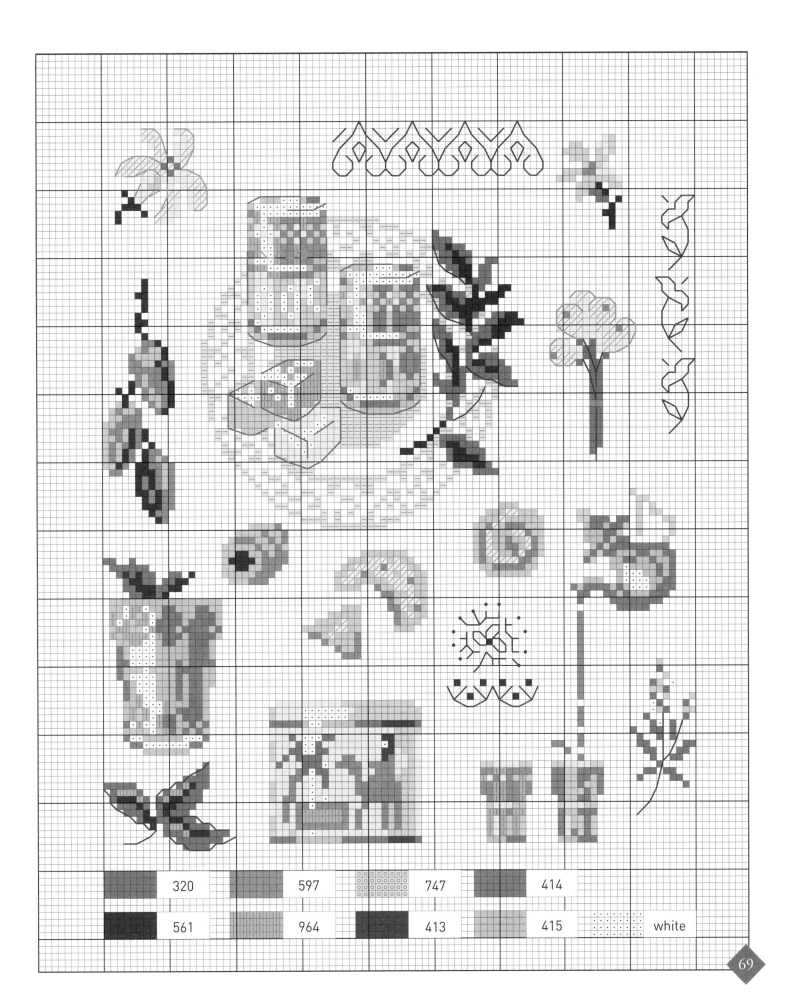

	320		597		747		414
	561		964		413		415

white

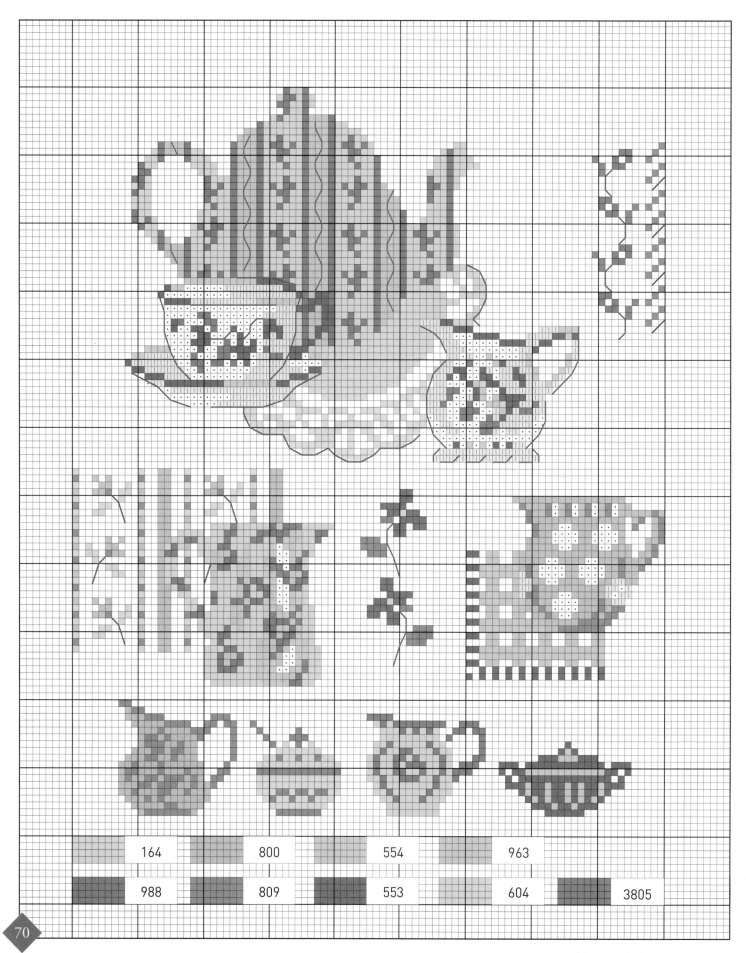

| | 164 | | 800 | | 554 | | 963 |
| | 988 | | 809 | | 553 | | 604 | | 3805 |

A photo of the top left design is on page 55.

	738		445		white		318
	433		436		726		3743		317

A photo of the center design is on page 55.

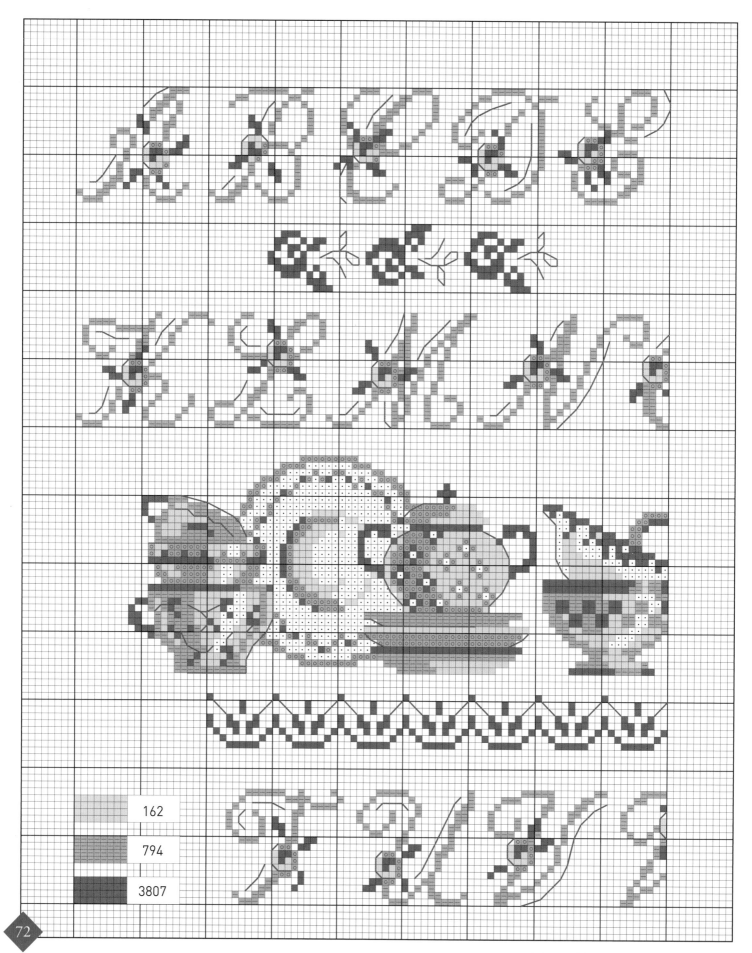

162

794

3807

A photo of the tea set border is on page 52.

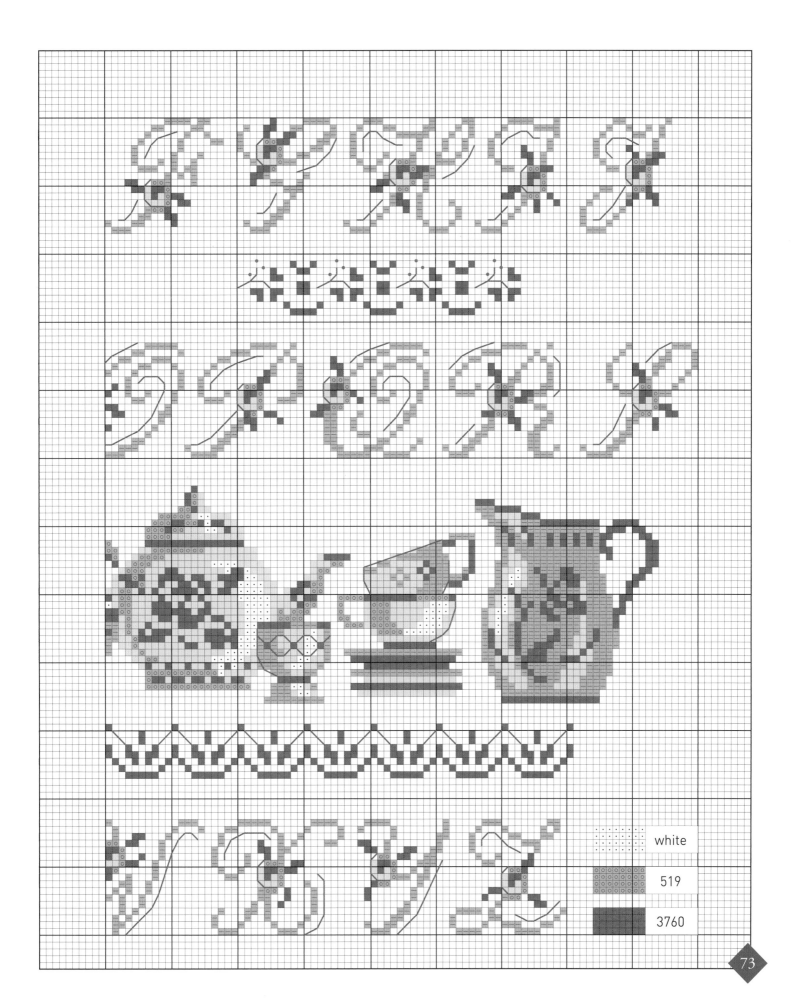

white

519

3760

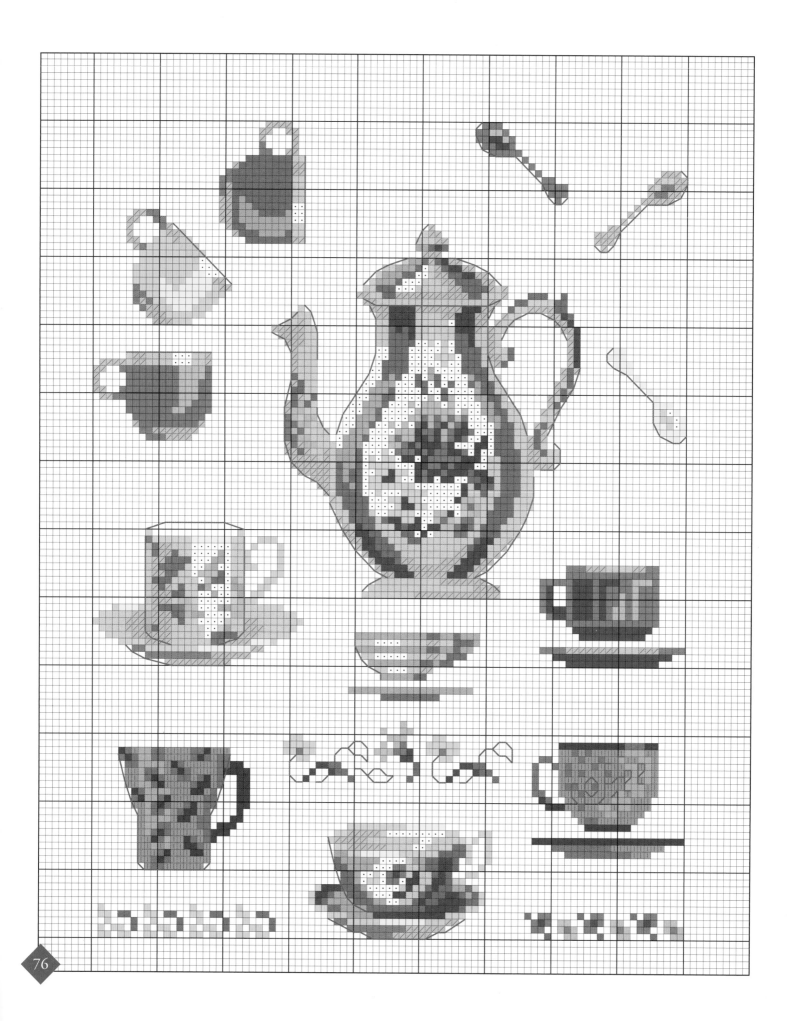

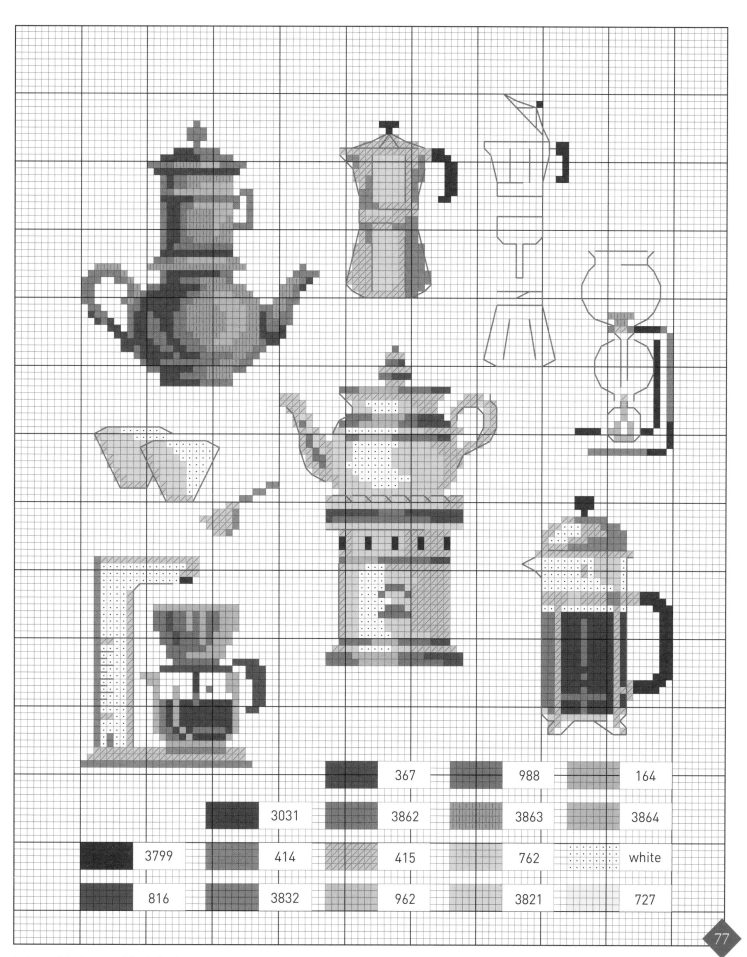

	367		988		164
	3031		3862		3863		3864
	3799		414		415		762		white
	816		3832		962		3821		727

A photo of the bottom right design is on page 74.

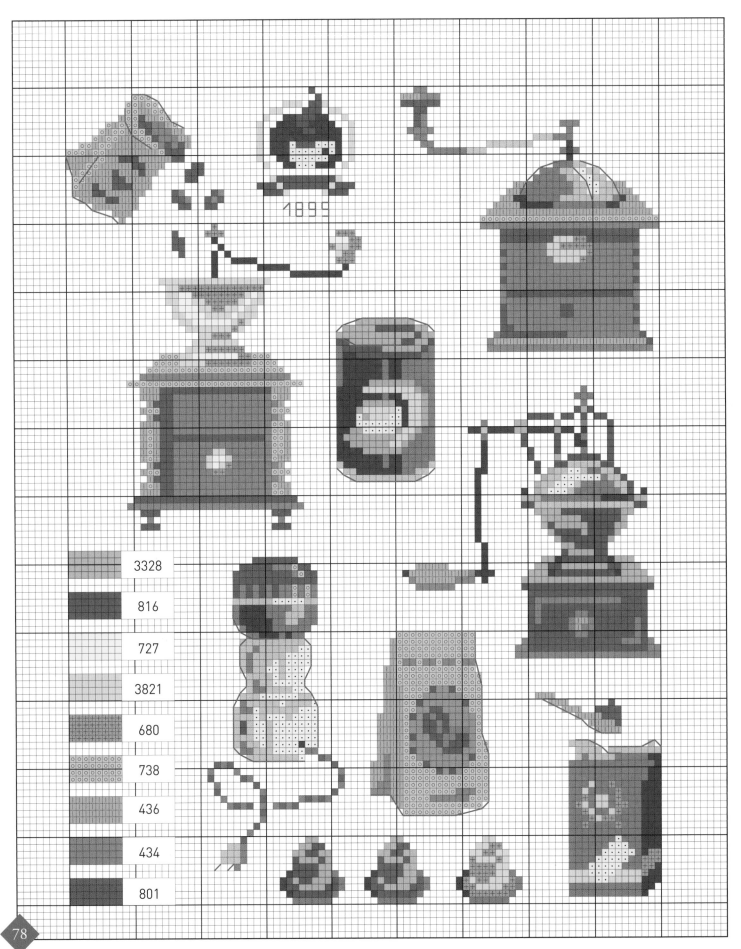

1895

	3328
	816
	727
	3821
	680
	738
	436
	434
	801

A photo of the bottom right design is on page 74.

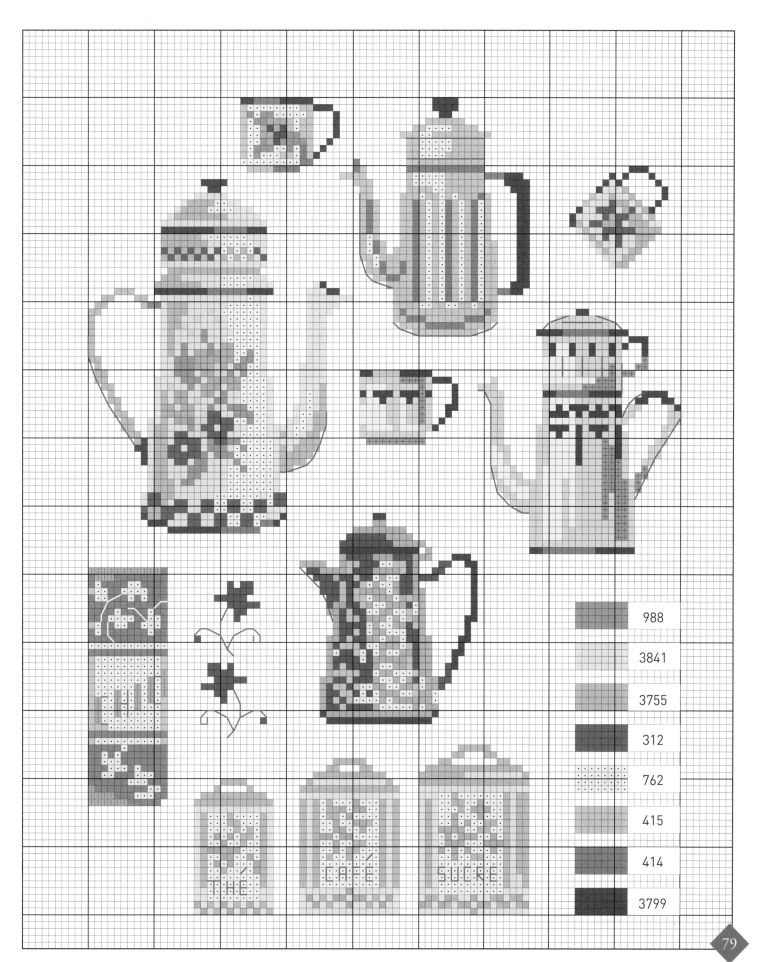

	988
	3841
	3755
	312
	762
	415
	414
	3799

A photo of the red coffeepot is on page 74.

| | 746 | | 677 | | 437 | | 435 | | 433 |
| | 3031 | | 840 | | 562 | | 563 | | 322 |

A photo of the top right design is on page 74.

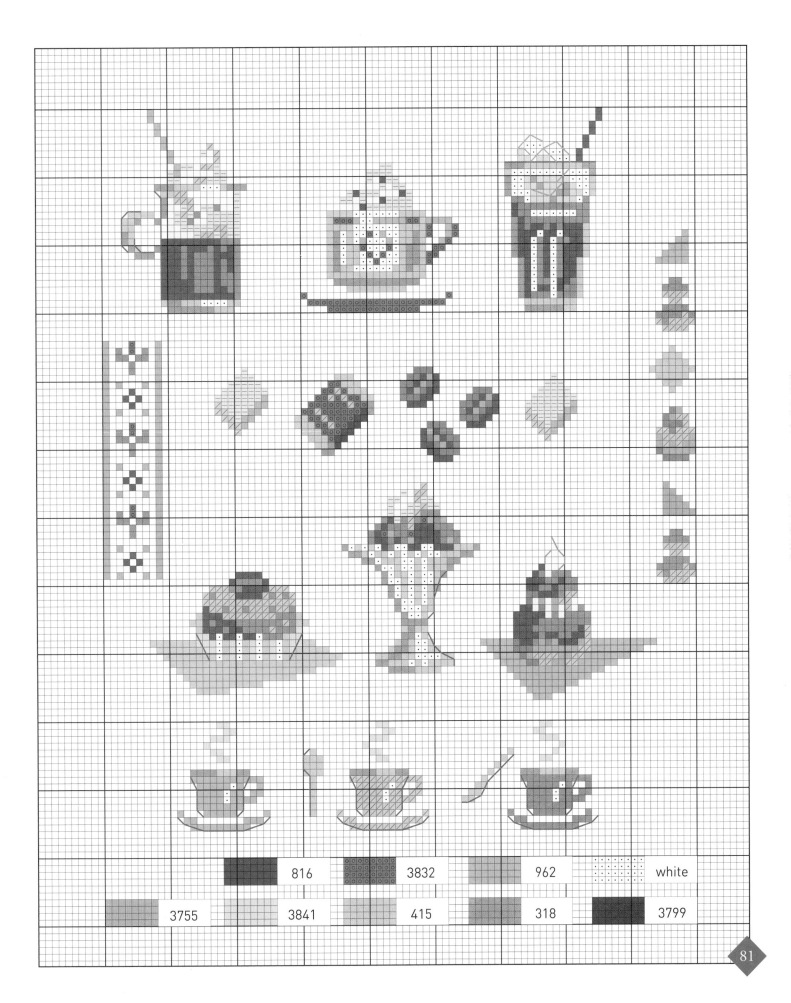

	816		3832		962		white
	3755		3841		415		318		3799

	738		436		434		3781		3831
	319		987		989		727		3821

A photo of the bottom right design is on page 74.

PETIT NOIR

MATIN

GRAND OU
PETIT
CRÈME
Noisette
ALLONGÉ

FRAPPÉ
OU
VIENNOIS

ESPRESSO

DÉCA
OU
SERRÉ

	712		842		311		597
	3799		317		318		415		white

| | 3862 | | 3031 | | 3712 | | 347 | | white |

A photo of this design is on page 75.

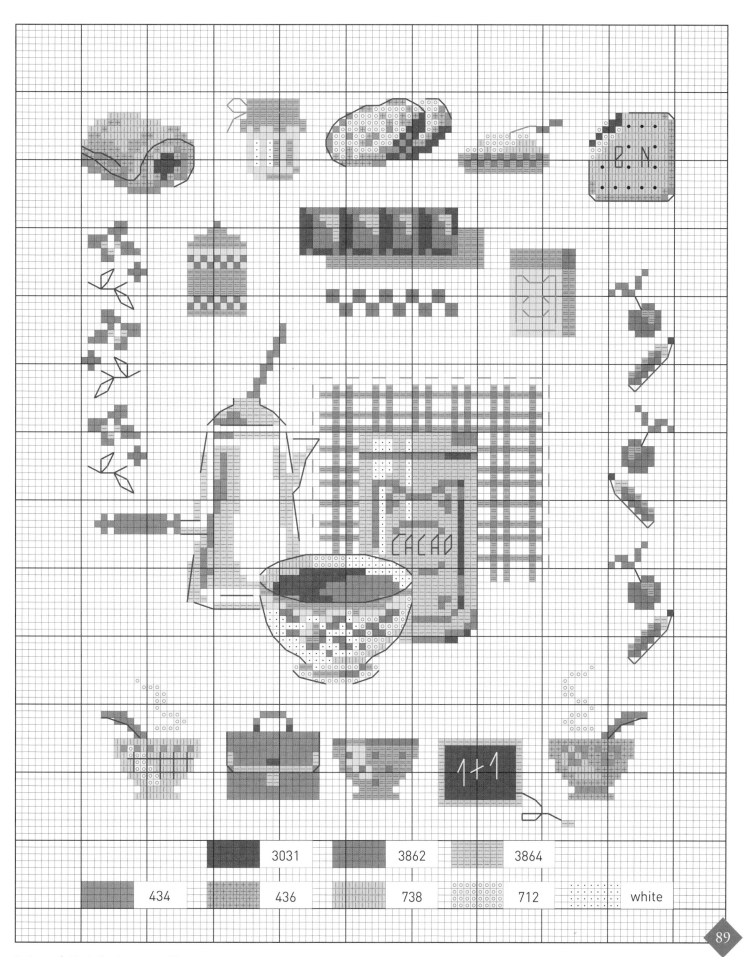

	3031		3862		3864
	434		436		738		712		white

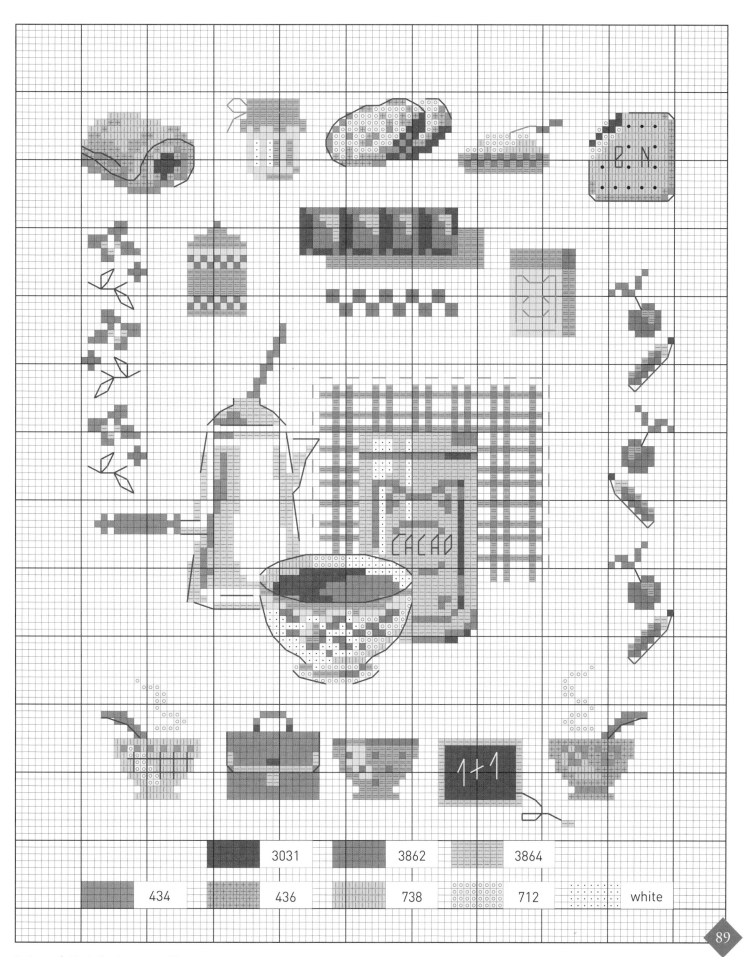

89

A photo of this design is on page 86.

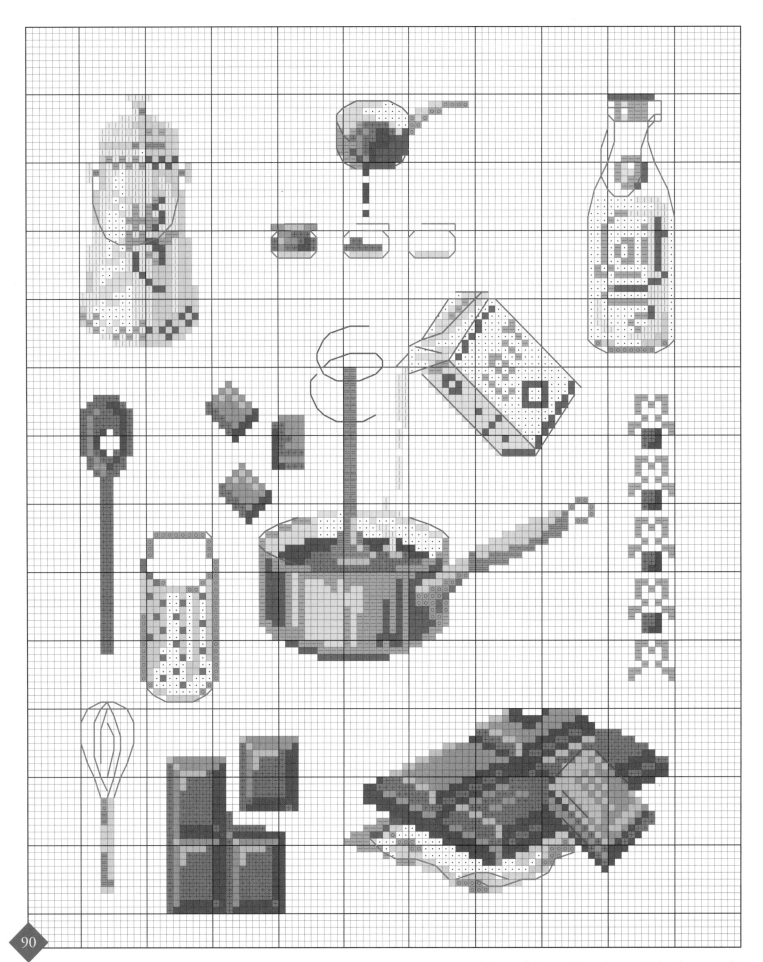

A photo of the top right and center designs is on page 87.

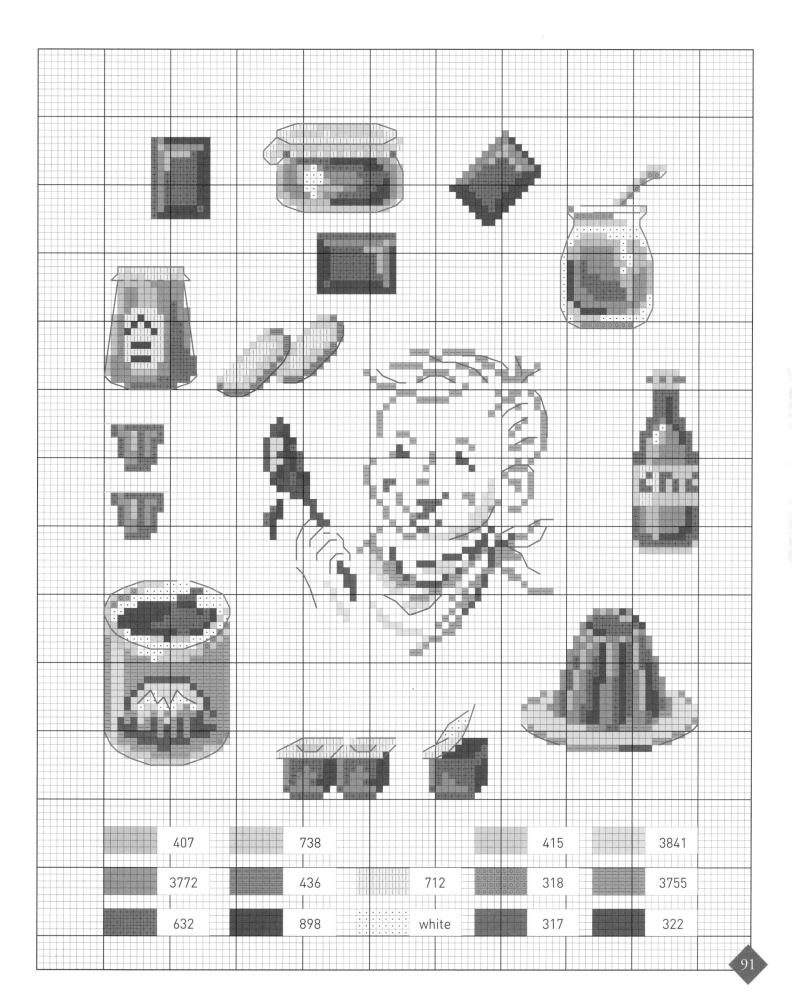

	407		738		415		3841
	3772		436		712		318		3755
	632		898		white		317		322

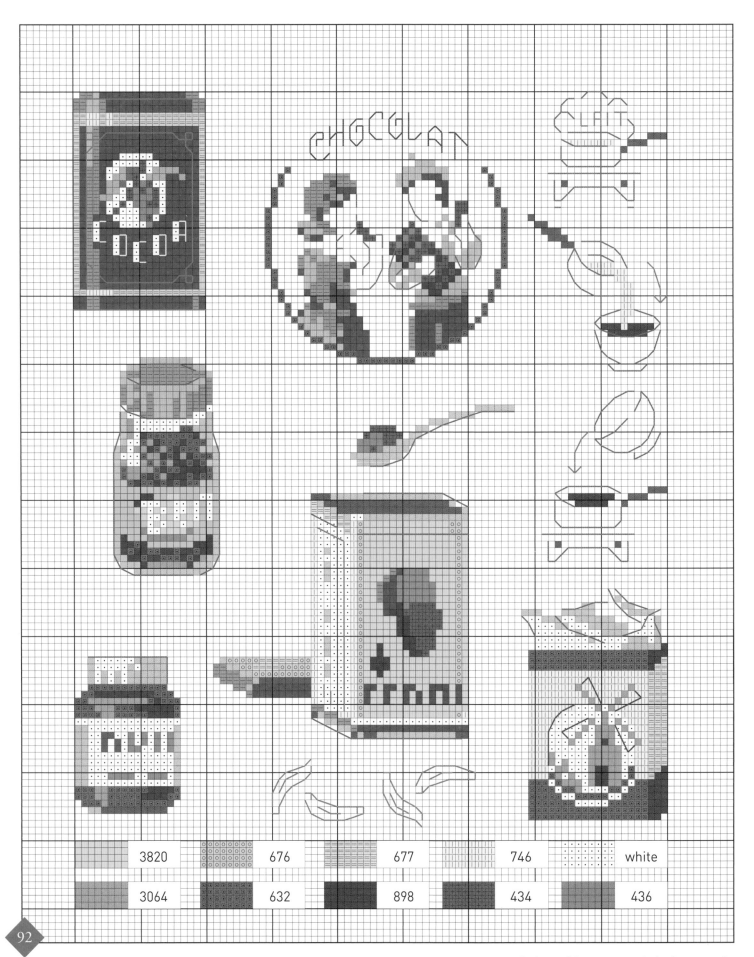

	3820		676		677		746		white
	3064		632		898		434		436

A photo of the top center design is on page 87.

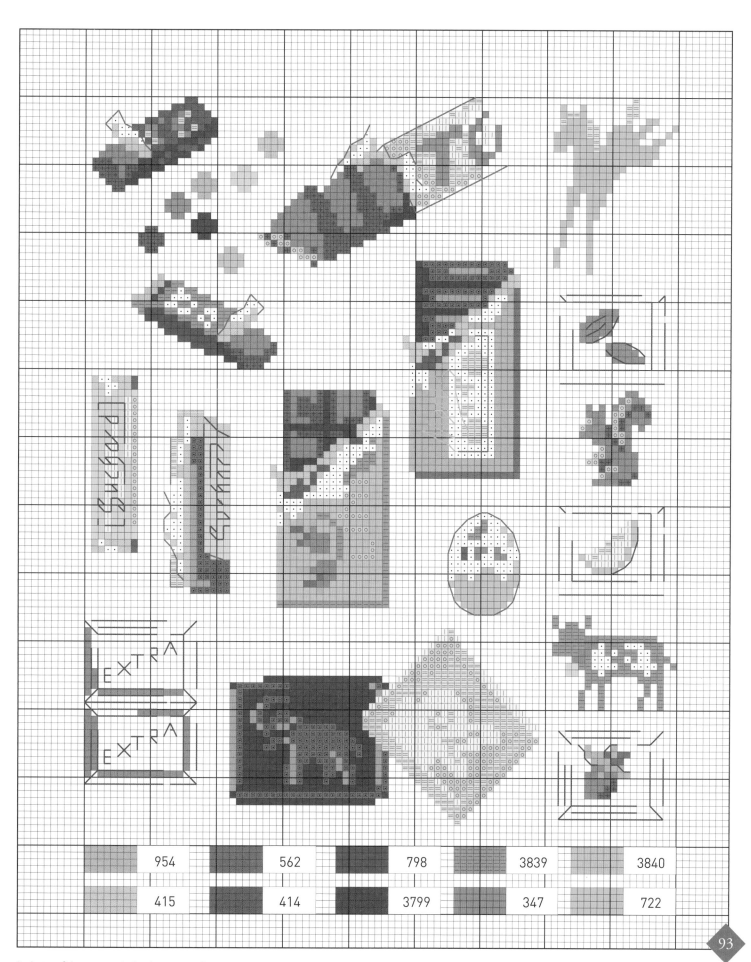

	954		562		798		3839		3840
	415		414		3799		347		722

A photo of the center design is on page 87.

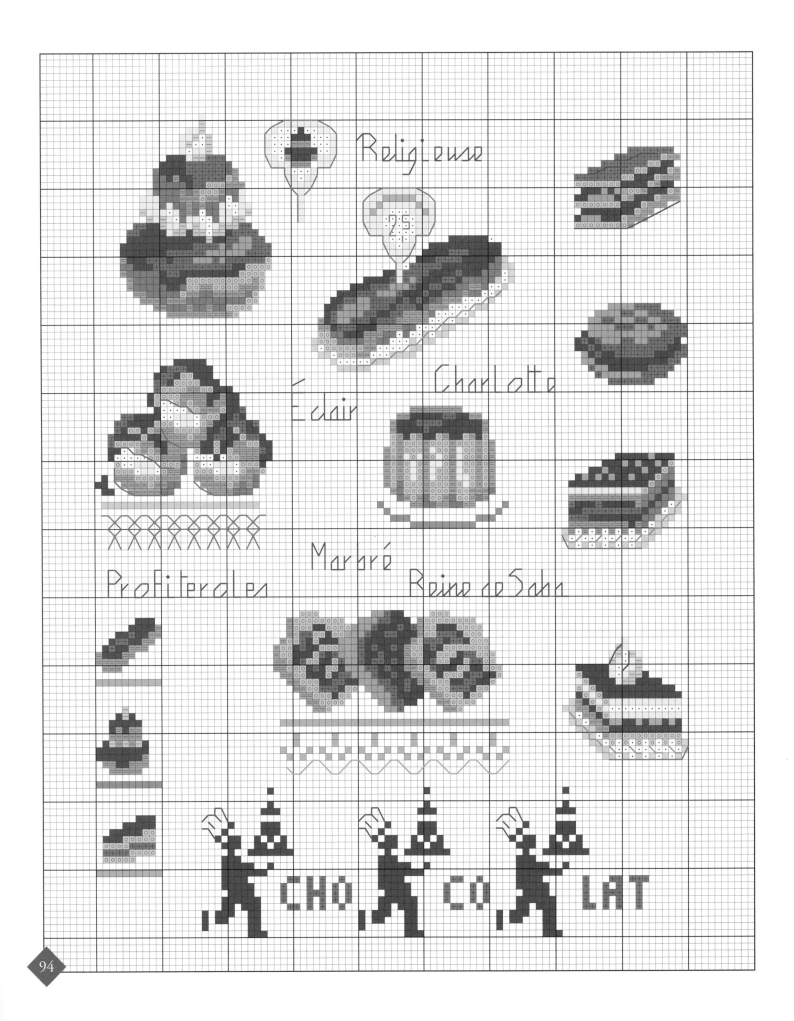

Religieuse

Charlotte

Éclair

Marbré

Profiteroles

Reine de Sahn

CHO CO LAT

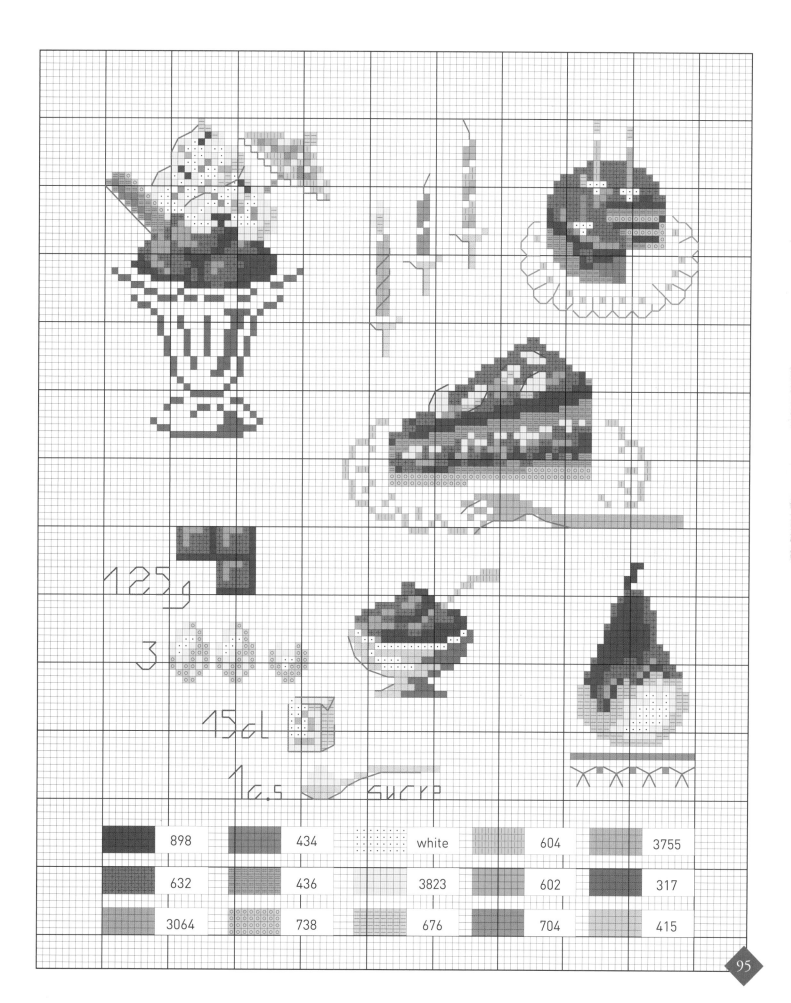

	898		434		white		604		3755
	632		436		3823		602		317
	3064		738		676		704		415

95

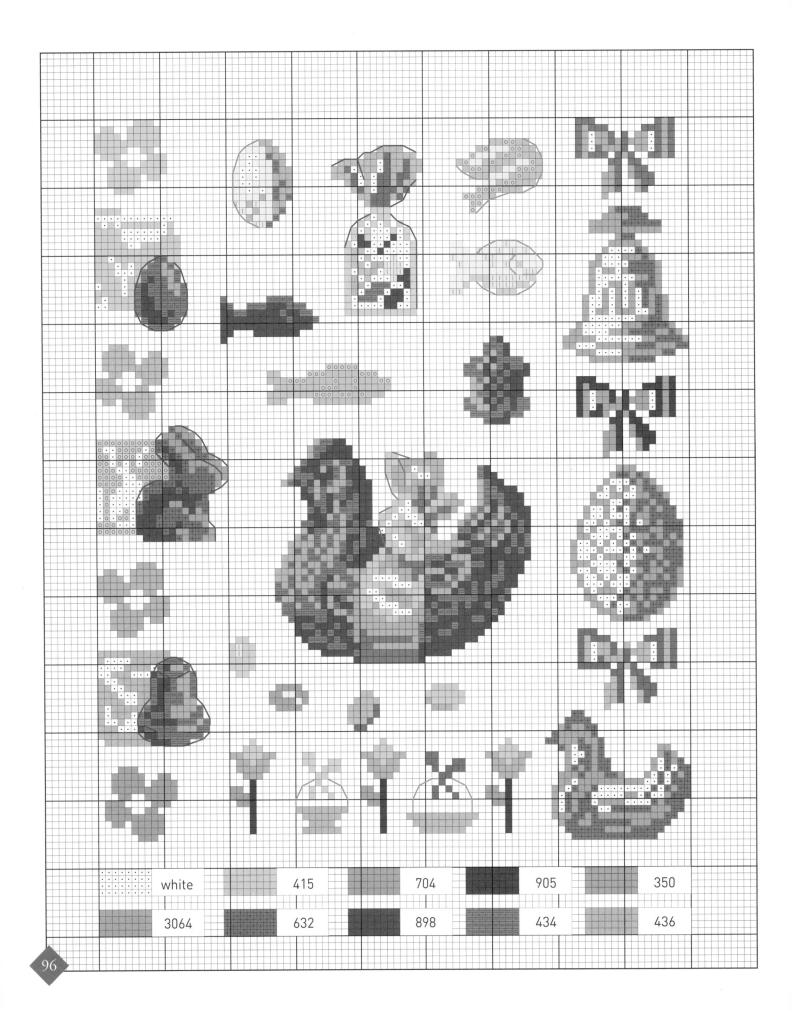

	white		415		704		905		350
	3064		632		898		434		436

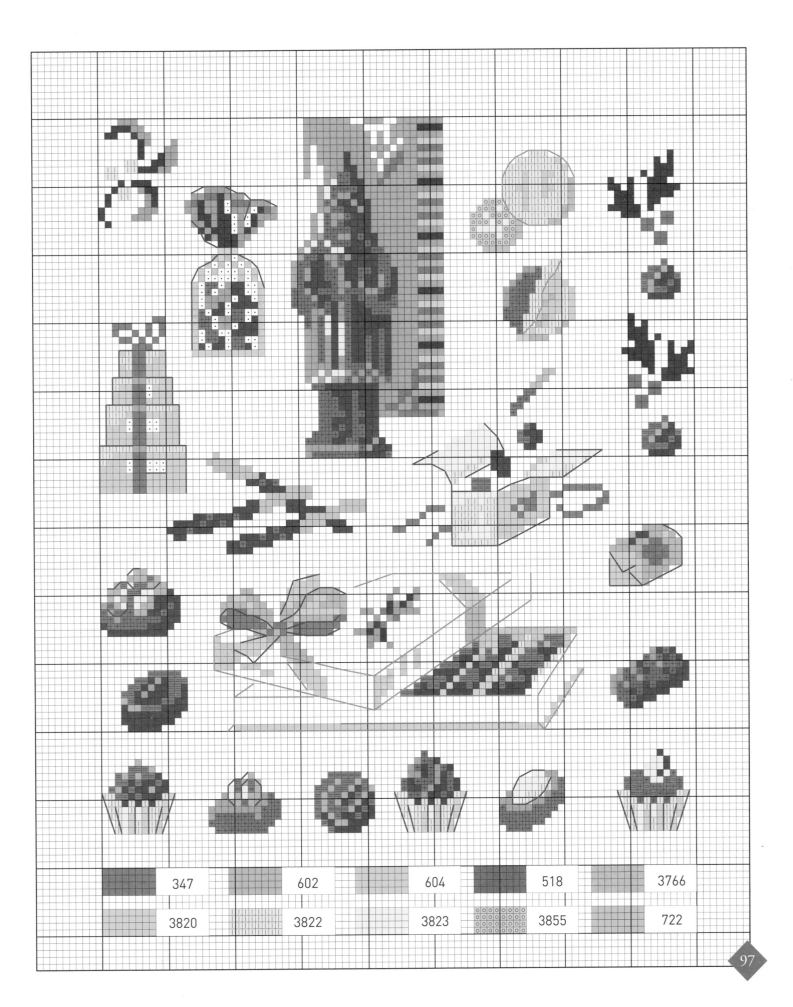

	347		602		604		518		3766
	3820		3822		3823		3855		722

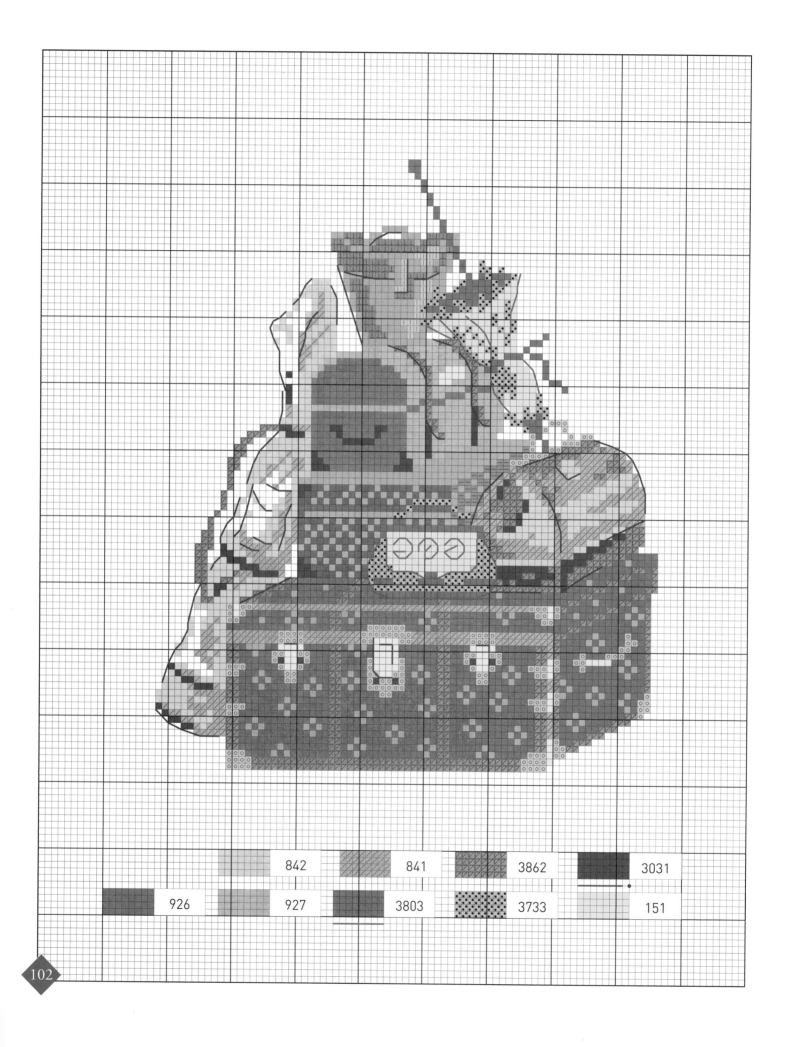

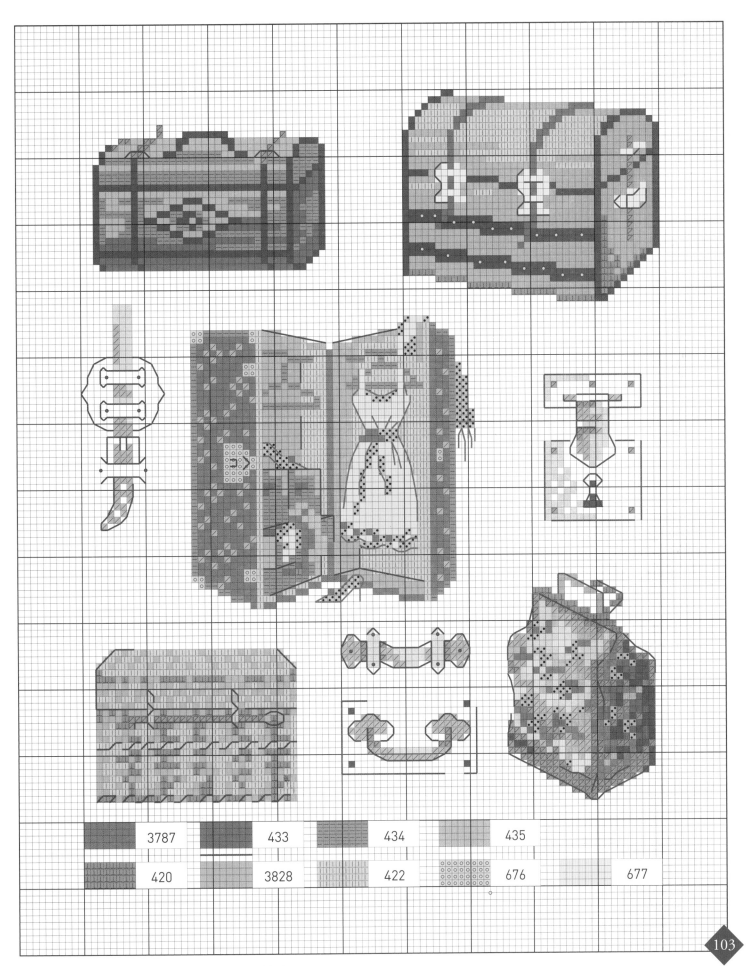

	3787		433		434		435
	420		3828		422		676		677

A photo of the trunk designs at top left and bottom right is on page 100.

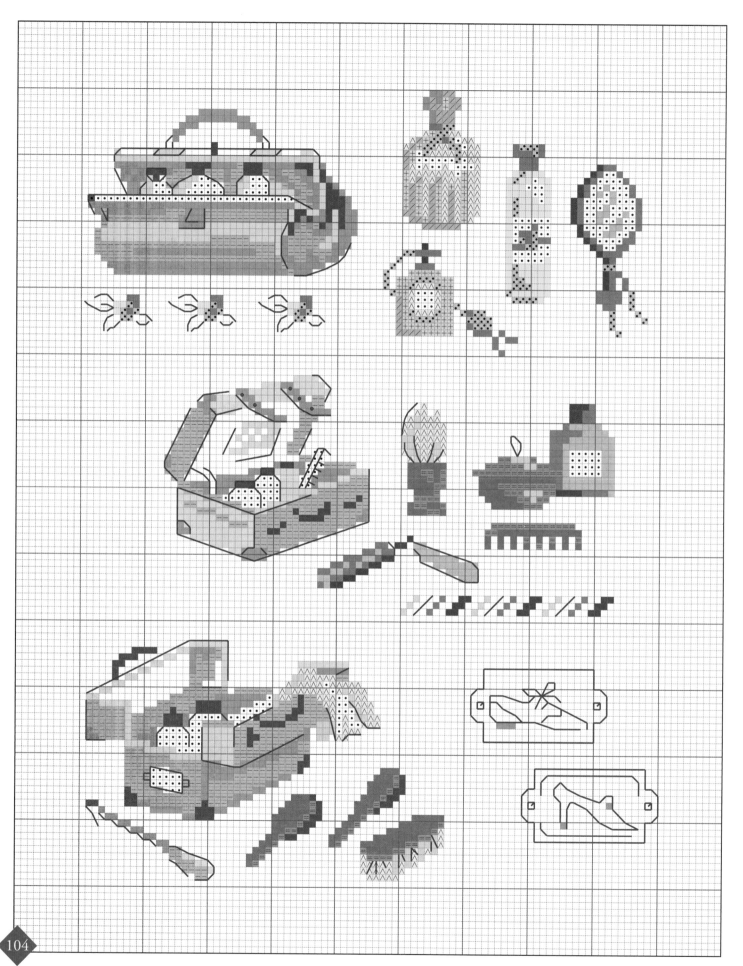

A photo of the two large scent bottles is on page 100.

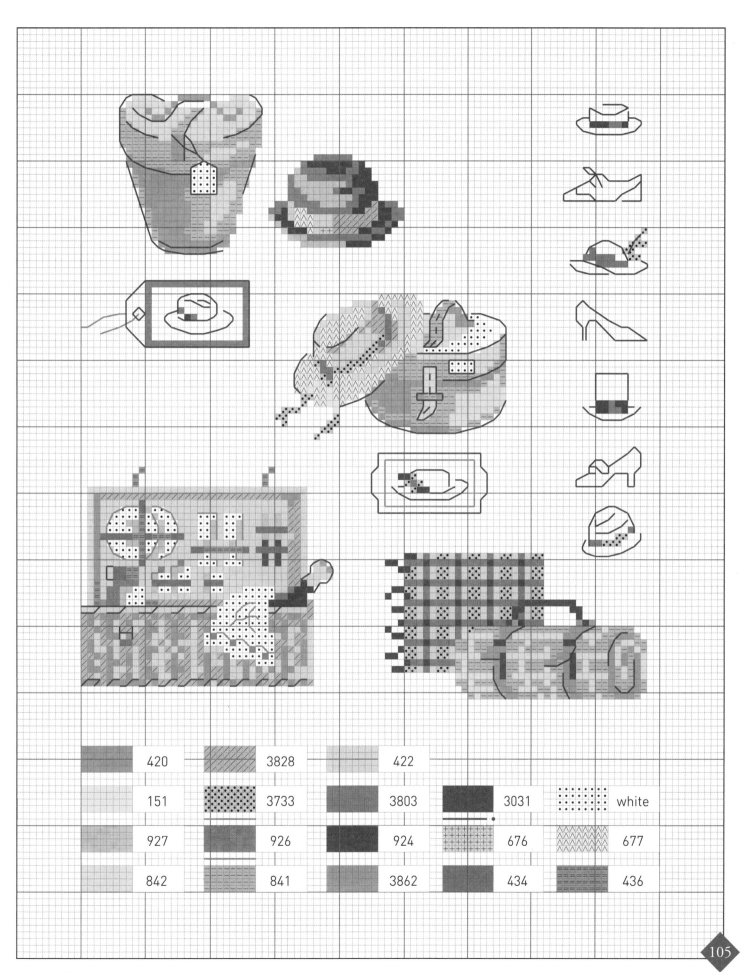

	420		3828		422				
	151		3733		3803		3031		white
	927		926		924		676		677
	842		841		3862		434		436

A photo of the small hatbox and the picnic basket is on page 100.

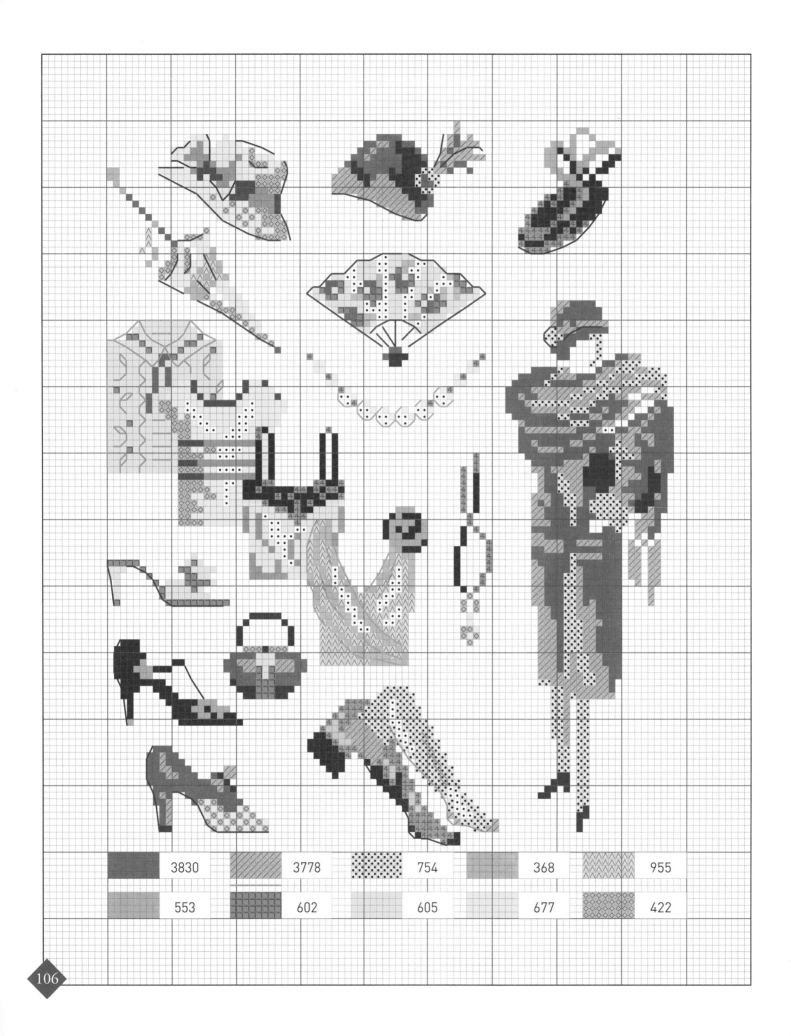

	3830		3778		754		368		955
	553		602		605		677		422

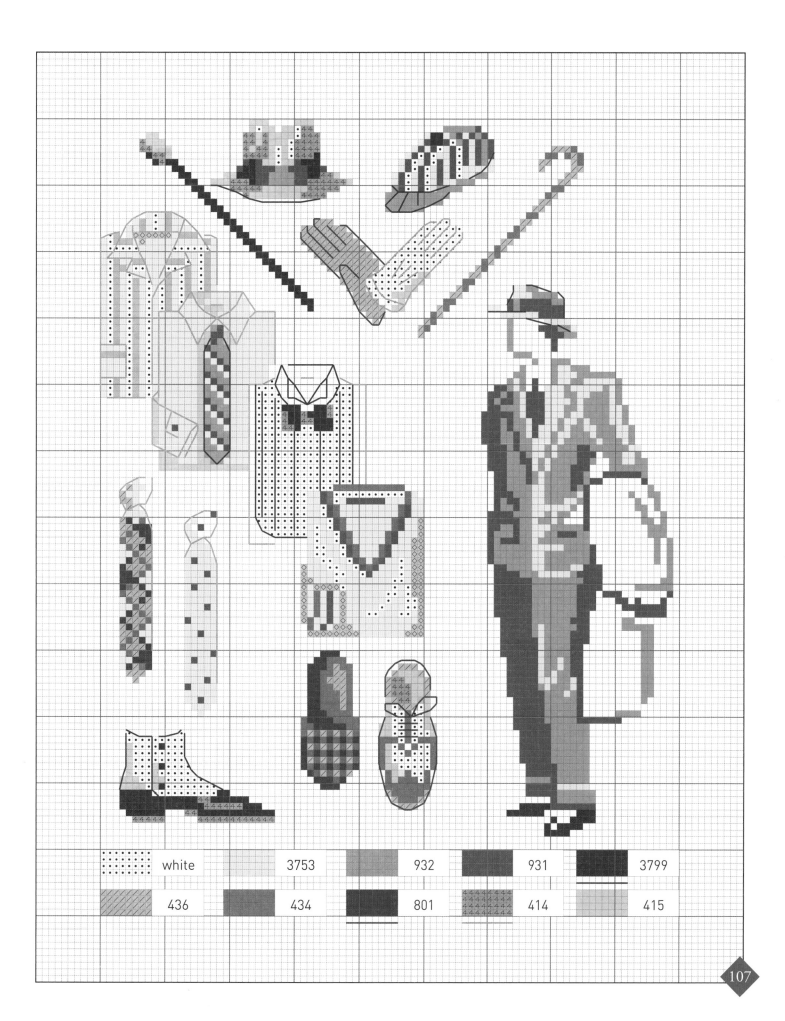

TRANSATLANTIQUE

CABINE

1ère

CLASSE

	347		351		434		437		739

·:·:·: white		3841		826		824		3799

A photo of the ship's wheel and the bottom design is on page 99.

677   437   435   729   676

A photo of this design is on page 98.

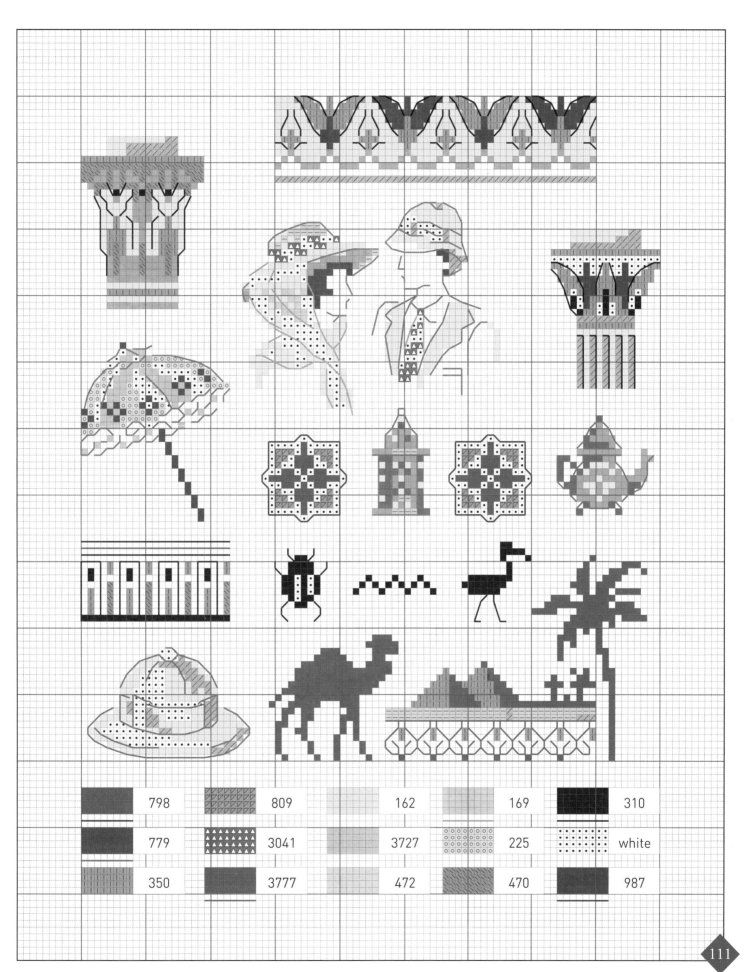

	798		809		162		169		310
	779		3041		3727		225		white
	350		3777		472		470		987

A photo of the parasol is on page 100.

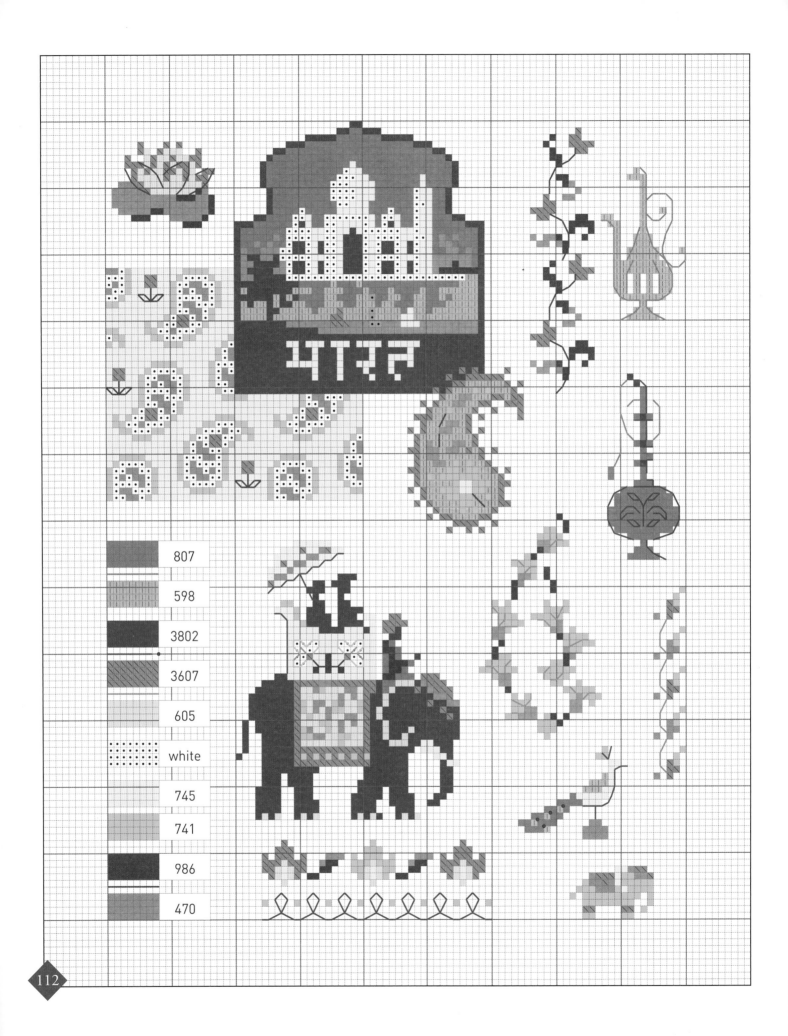

309
935
801
3346
435
471

POSTE 40

114

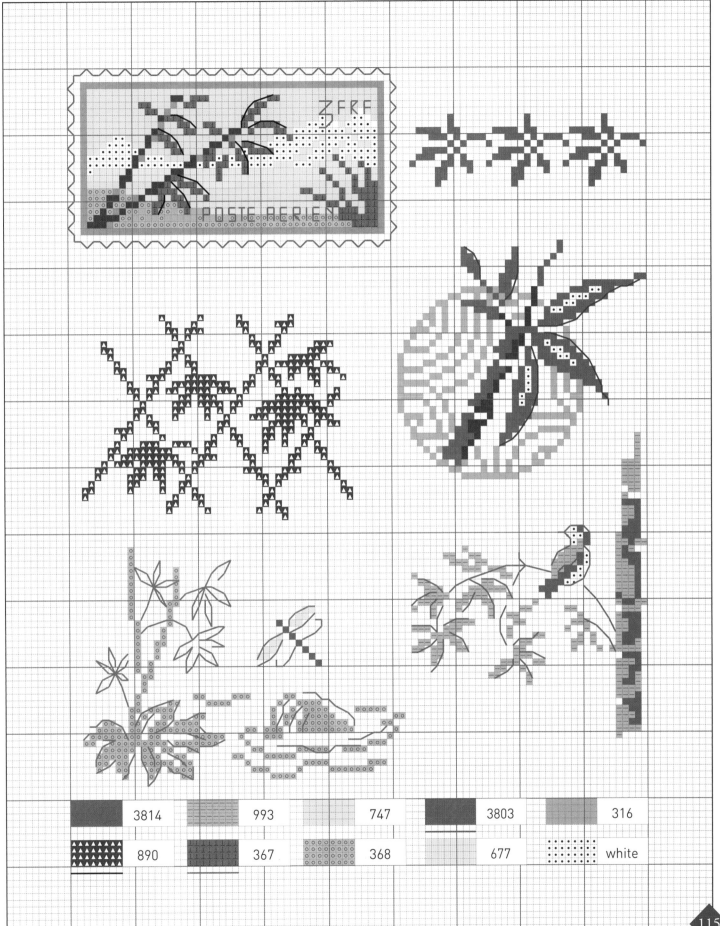

	3814		993		747		3803		316
	890		367		368		677		white

115

	798		809		3761		321		3801

A photo of the snowflakes and the skaters is on page 101.

A photo of the top center medallion and the skier is on page 101.

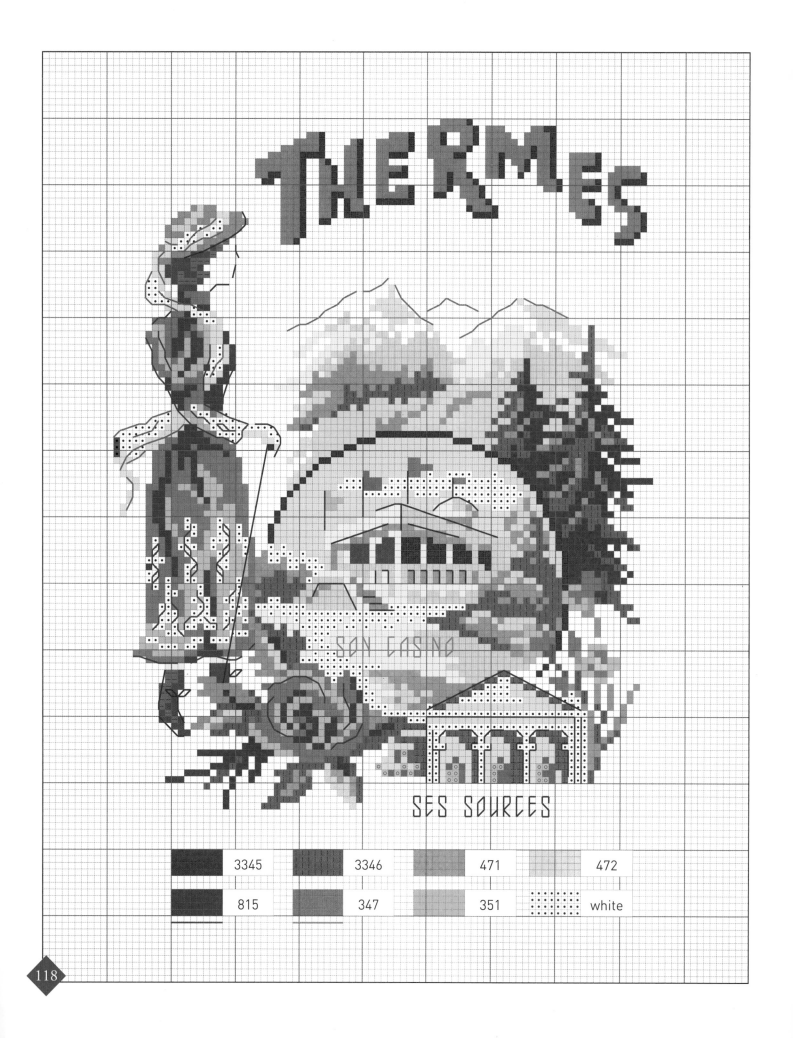

THERMES

SON CASINO

SES SOURCES

	3345		3346		471		472
	815		347		351		white

Programme

Bain d'air du matin

Visite aux sources

Excursions à la carte

Concert au kiosque du Casino

Soirée théâtrale

	745		676		436		434		779
	162		3766		518		931		310

BUDAPEST
CONSTANTINOPLE
ORIENT
EXPRESS

CHEMIN DE FER
DU NORD ET DE L'EST

TRAIN RAPIDE
1º ET 2º CLASSES

LONDRES – PARIS – VENISE

	161		334		3325		775		white

A photo of this design is on page 120.

	677		422		167		782		3854
	351		349		470		563		932

	317		white		420		437		739

127

435

301

3857

312

826

827

A photo of the bottom left design is on page 121.

Soirée de Gala

	987		989		772		3799		414
	729		676		677		white		415
	150		961		604		963		754

3820		3822		745		304		350

Typography is used for the text on page 121.

	680		3821		745
	3849		163		564		3857		150

A photo of the Chinese lanterns and vase (left) is on page 133.

	3841	334	312
350	604	818	white	310

A photo of the geisha, butterfly, teapot, and branch in flower is on page 133.

| | 632 | | 3859 | | 402 | | 986 | | 988 |
| | 833 | | 3821 | | 745 | | 816 | | 350 |

A photo of this design is on page 132.

МОСКВА

ИКРА

	310		317		318		415		white
	3806		818		800		809		798

	3755		826		797		989		987

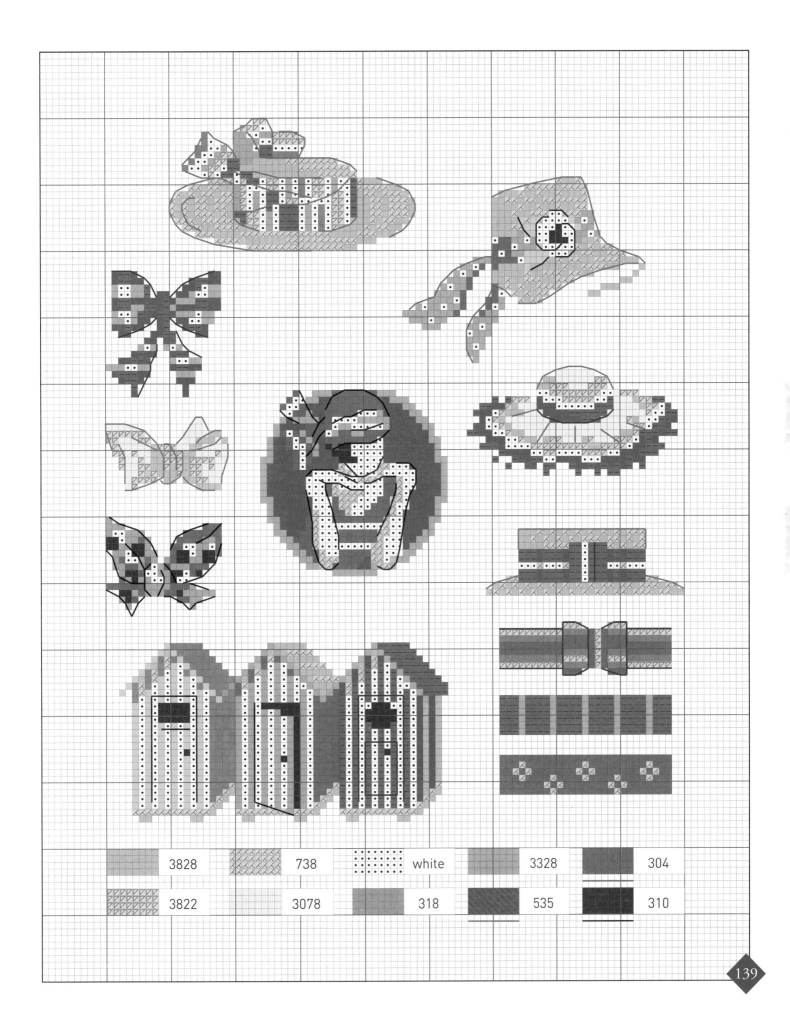

	3828		738		white		3328		304
	3822		3078		318		535		310

139

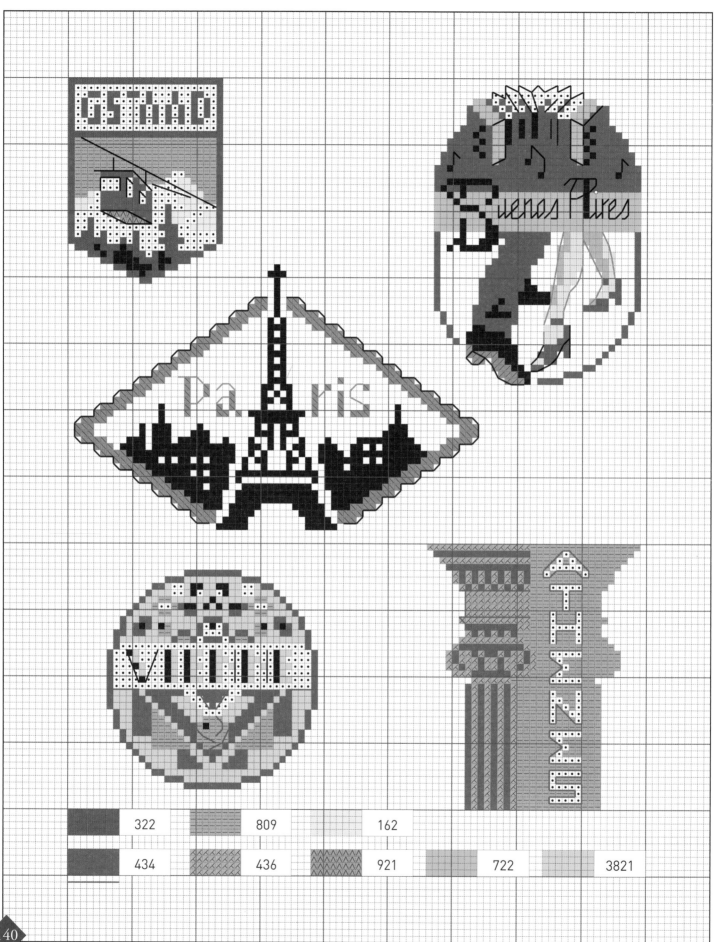

| | 322 | | 809 | | 162 | | | |
| | 434 | | 436 | | 921 | | 722 | | 3821 |

white	318	317	310
932	563	562	818
152	347		

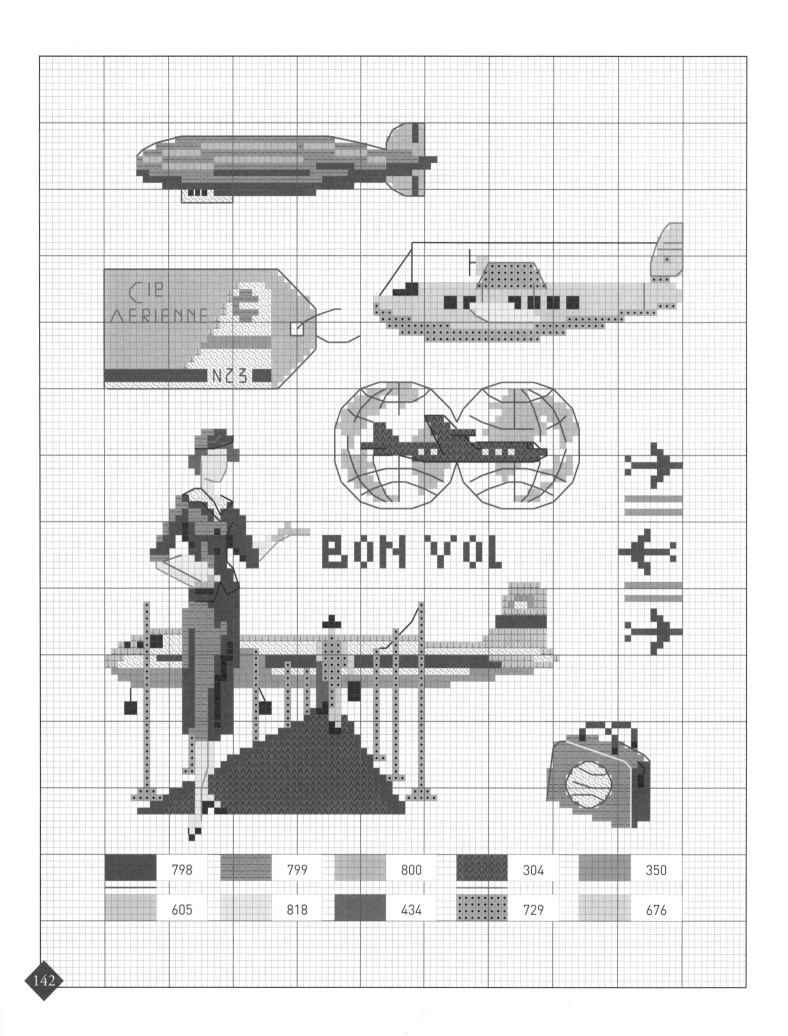

| | 798 | | 799 | | 800 | | 304 | | 350 |
| | 605 | | 818 | | 434 | | 729 | | 676 |

PREMIERE CLASSE

Bienvenue

PAR AVION

| 745 | white | 415 | 414 | 3799 |

Costumes Parisiens

1828

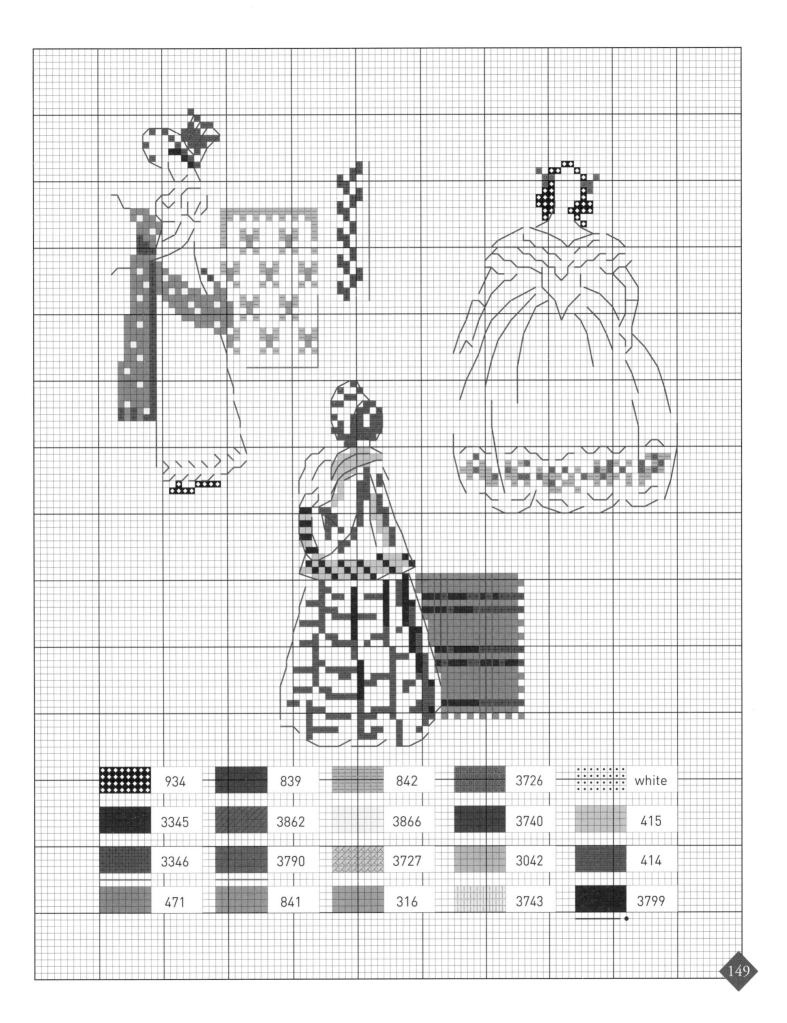

	934		839		842		3726		white
	3345		3862		3866		3740		415
	3346		3790		3727		3042		414
	471		841		316		3743		3799

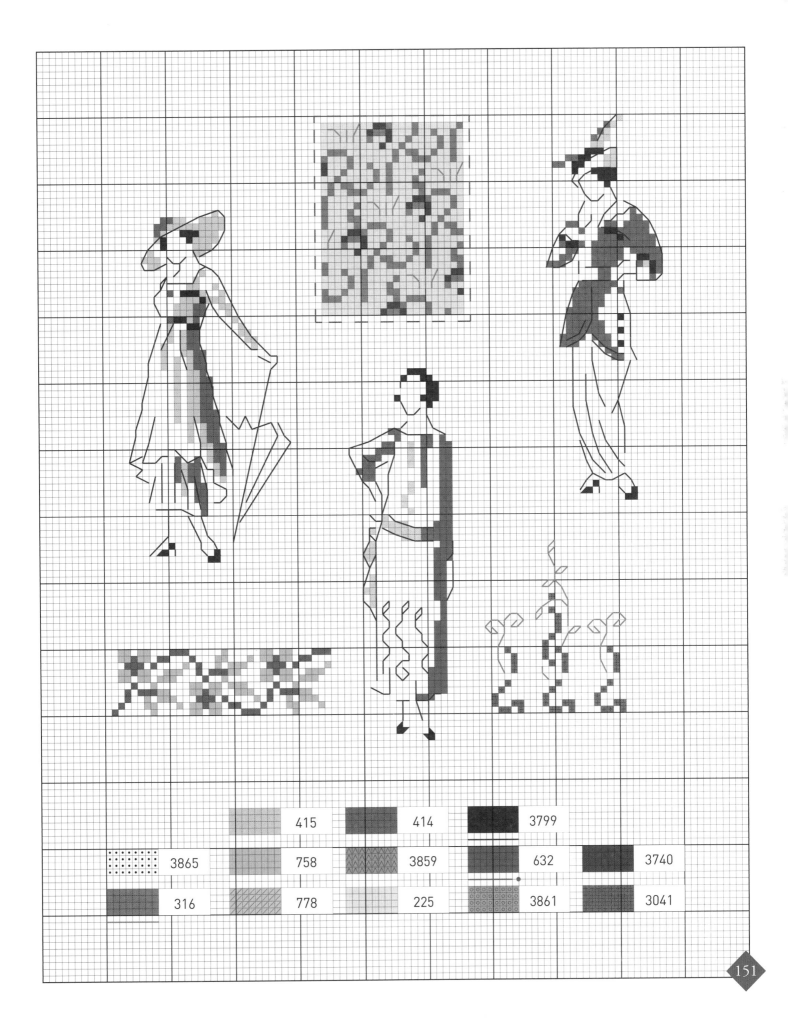

415

414

3799

3865

758

3859

632

3740

316

778

225

3861

3041

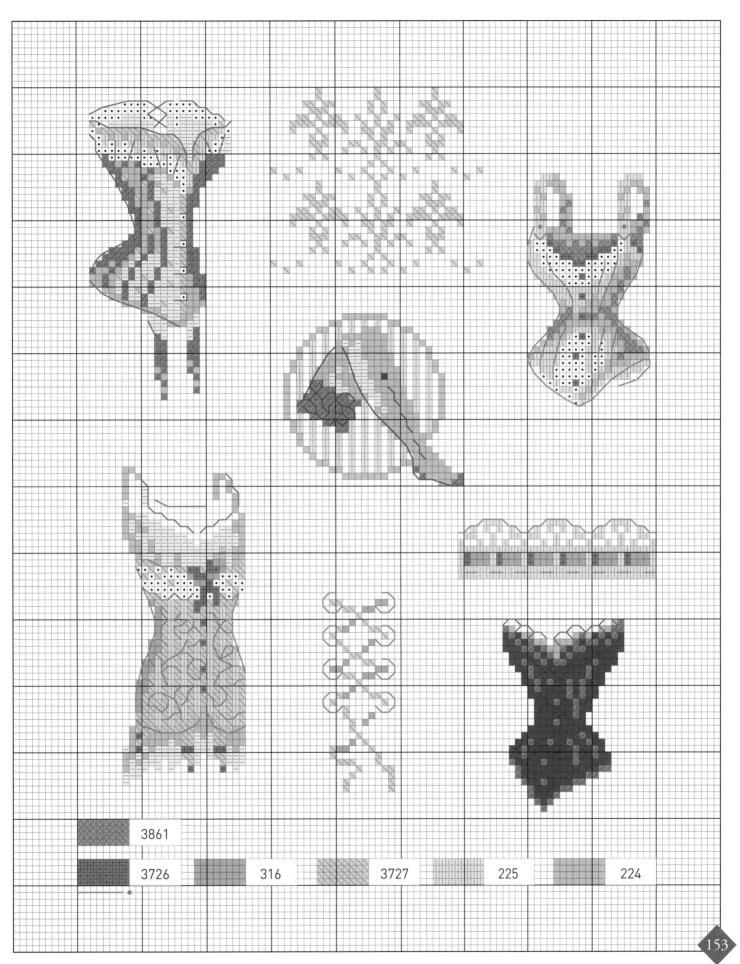

3861

3726 316 3727 225 224

A photo of some of these designs is on page 145.

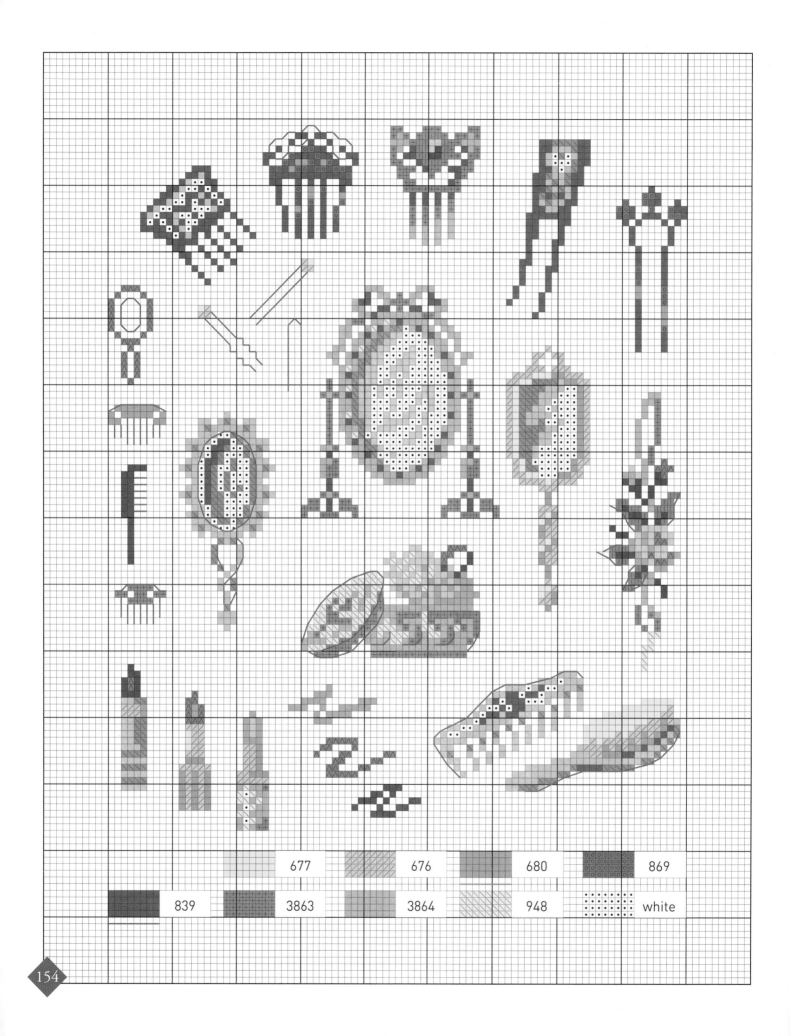

	677		676		680		869
	839		3863		3864		948		white

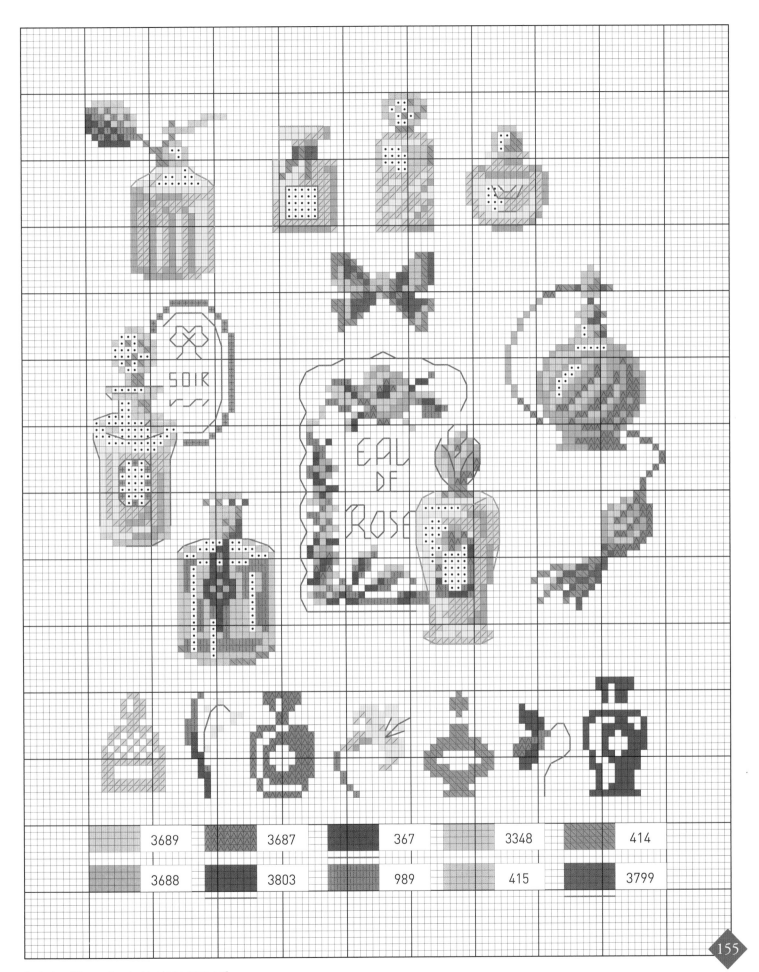

155

A photo of the center designs is on page 146.

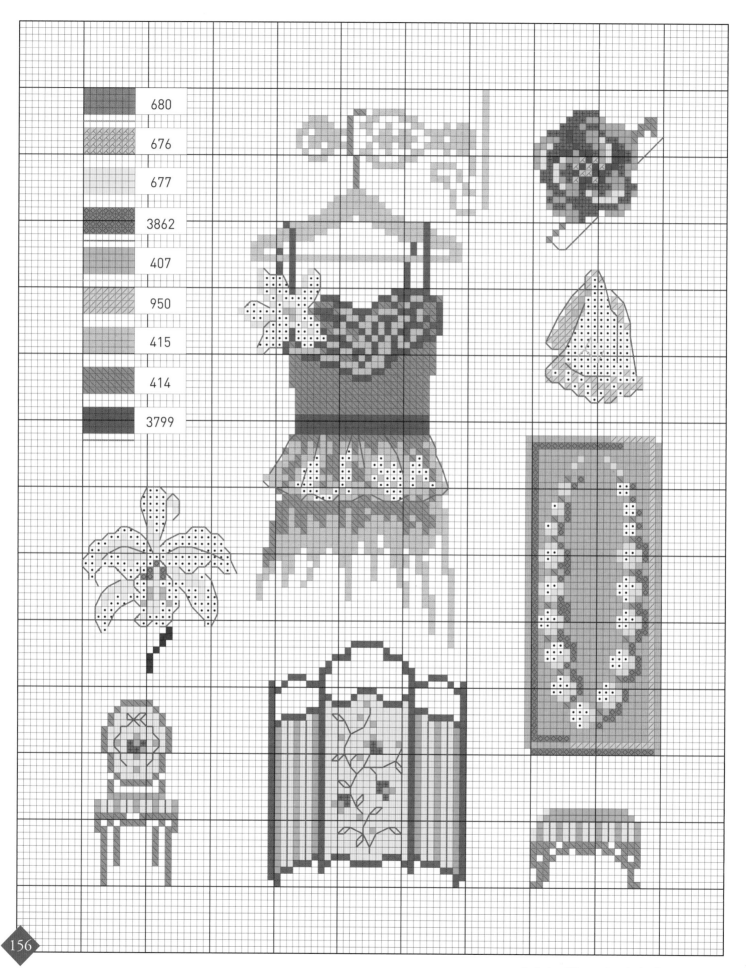

	680
	676
	677
	3862
	407
	950
	415
	414
	3799

A photo of the center design is on page 144.

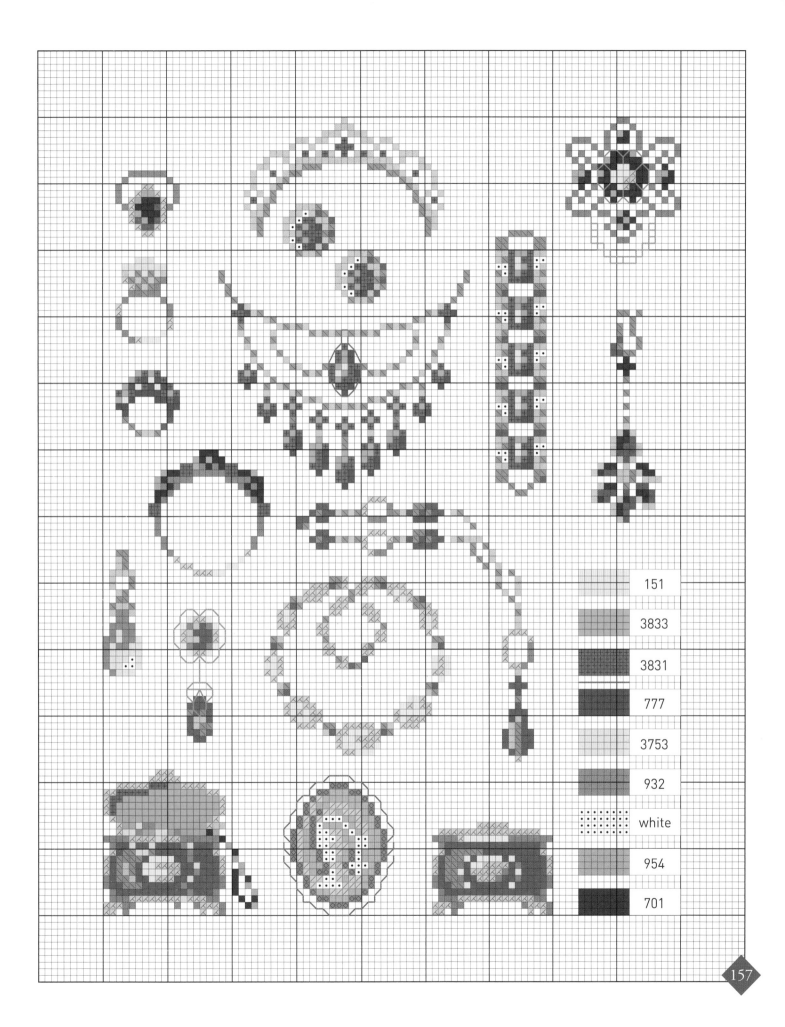

151

3833

3831

777

3753

932

white

954

701

157

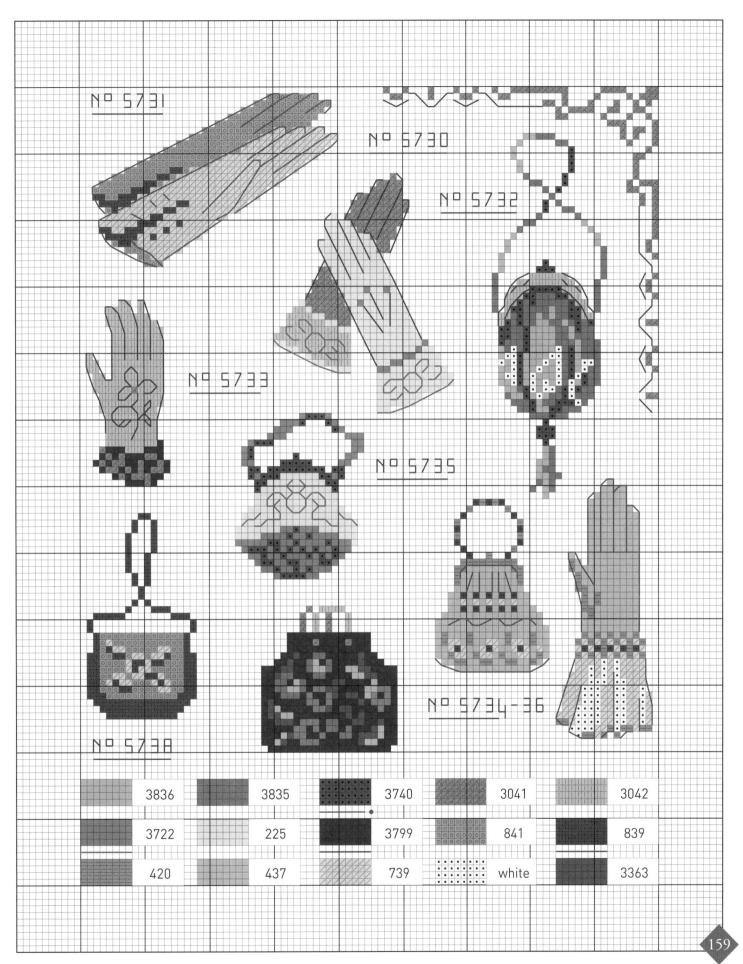

	3836		3835		3740		3041		3042
	3722		225		3799		841		839
	420		437		739		white		3363

A photo of the top designs is on page 147.

159

CHAPEAUX

	989
676	3828
779	3858

778	316	3726	3753	932

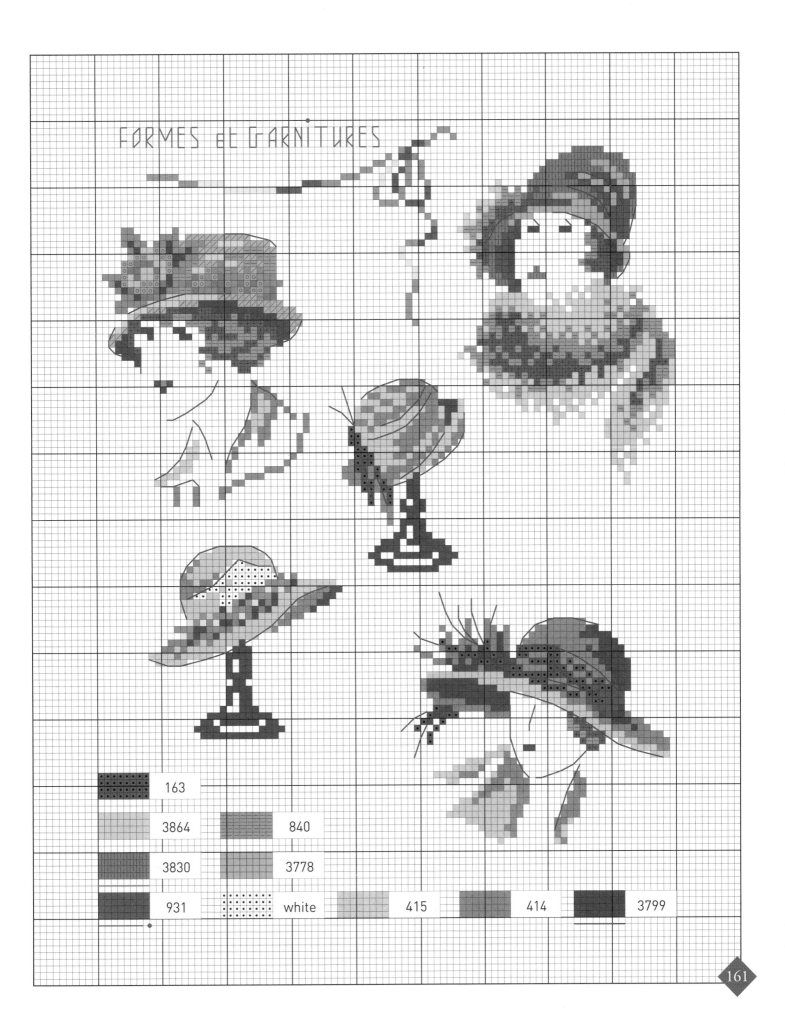

FORMES et GARNITURES

163		
3864	840	
3830	3778	
931	white	415	414	3799

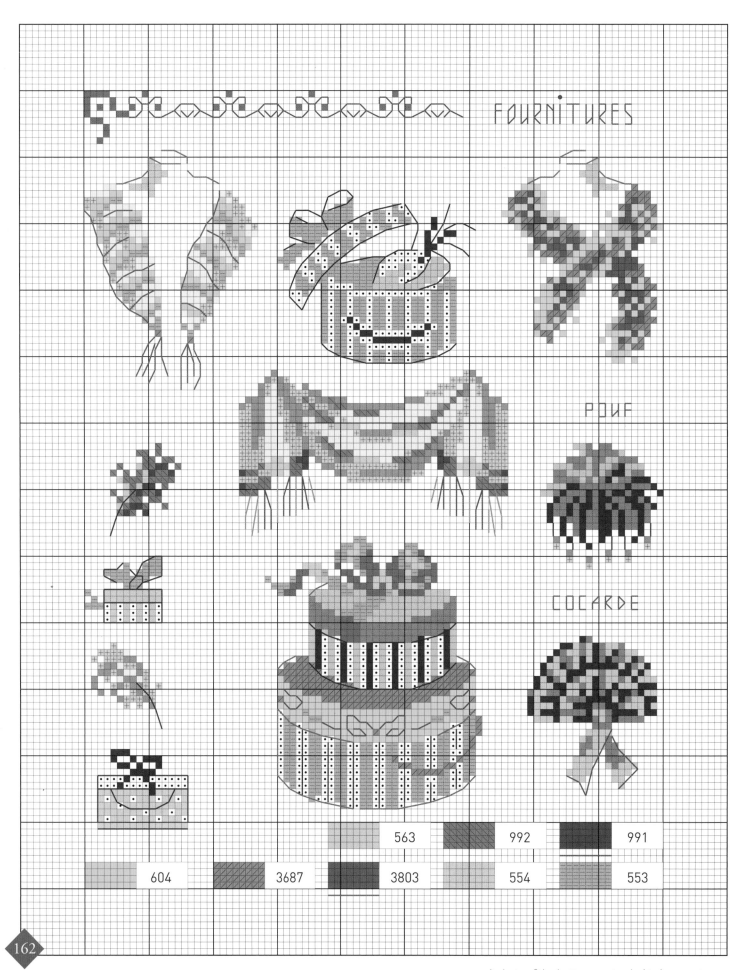

FOURNITURES

POUF

COCARDE

		563		992		991
	604		3687		3803		554		553

A photo of the bottom center design is on page 147.

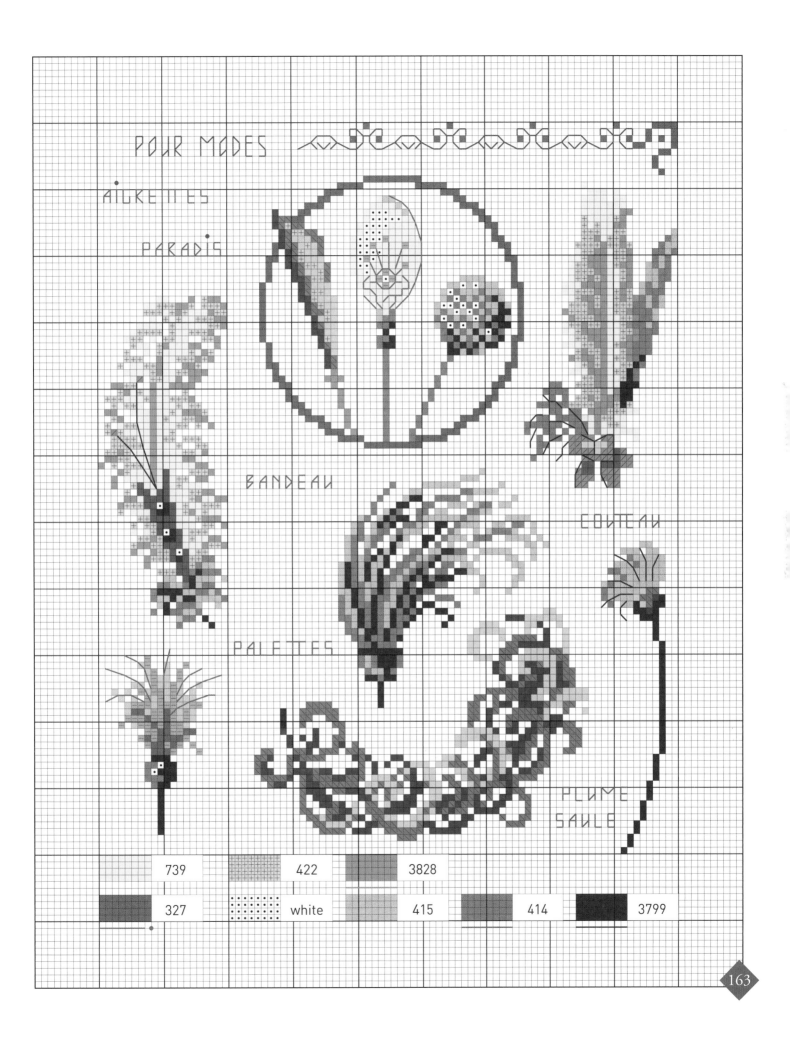

POUR MODES

AIGRETTES

PARADIS

BANDEAU

CONTEAU

PALETTES

PLUME
SAULE

	739		422		3828
	327		white		415		414		3799

163

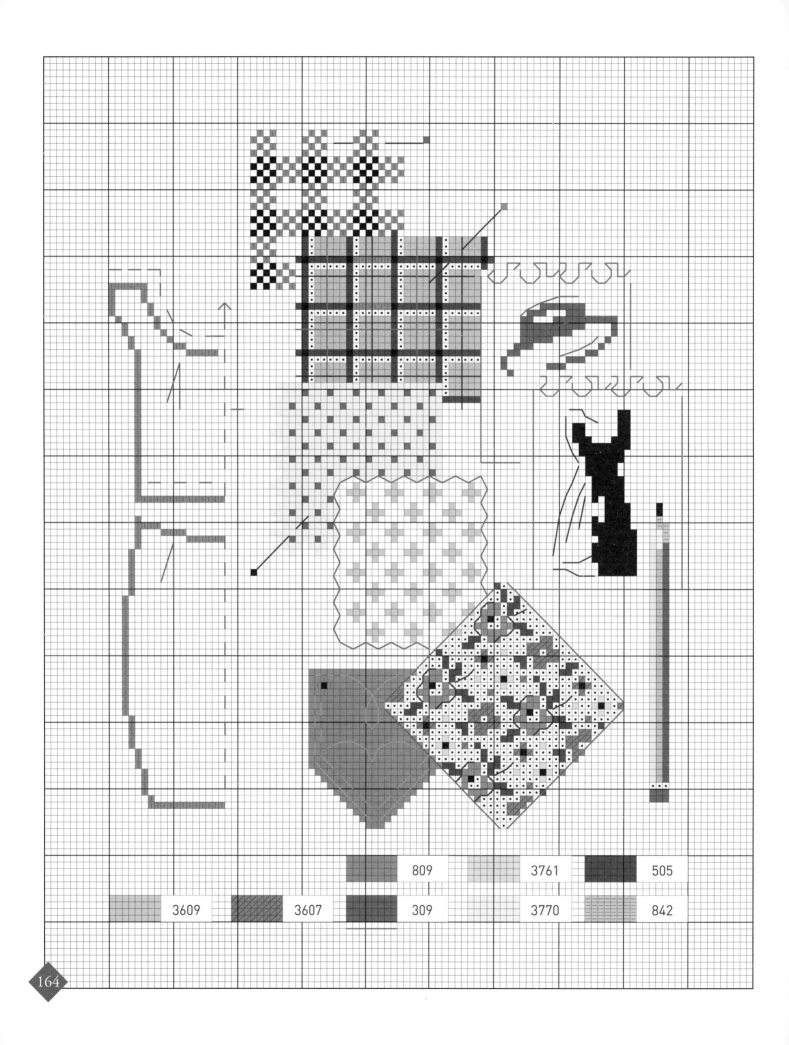

	809		3761		505
3609		3607		309		3770		842

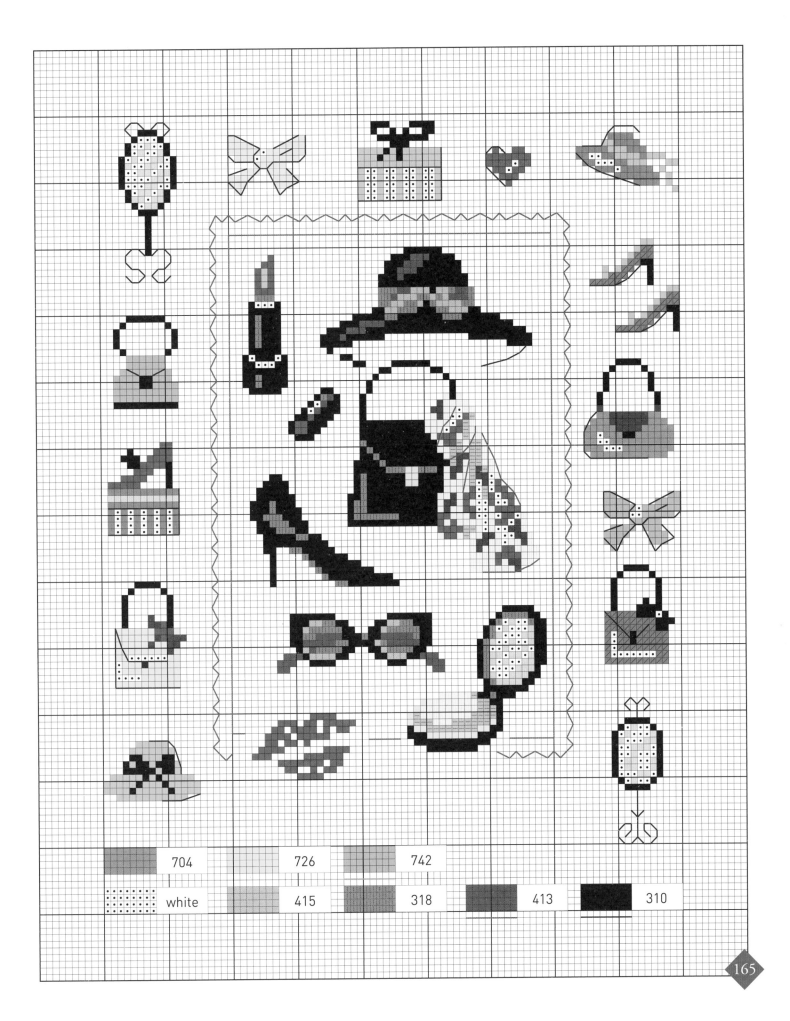

	704		726		742
white		415		318	

	413		310

A photo of these designs is on page 167.

A photo of the top design is on page 167.

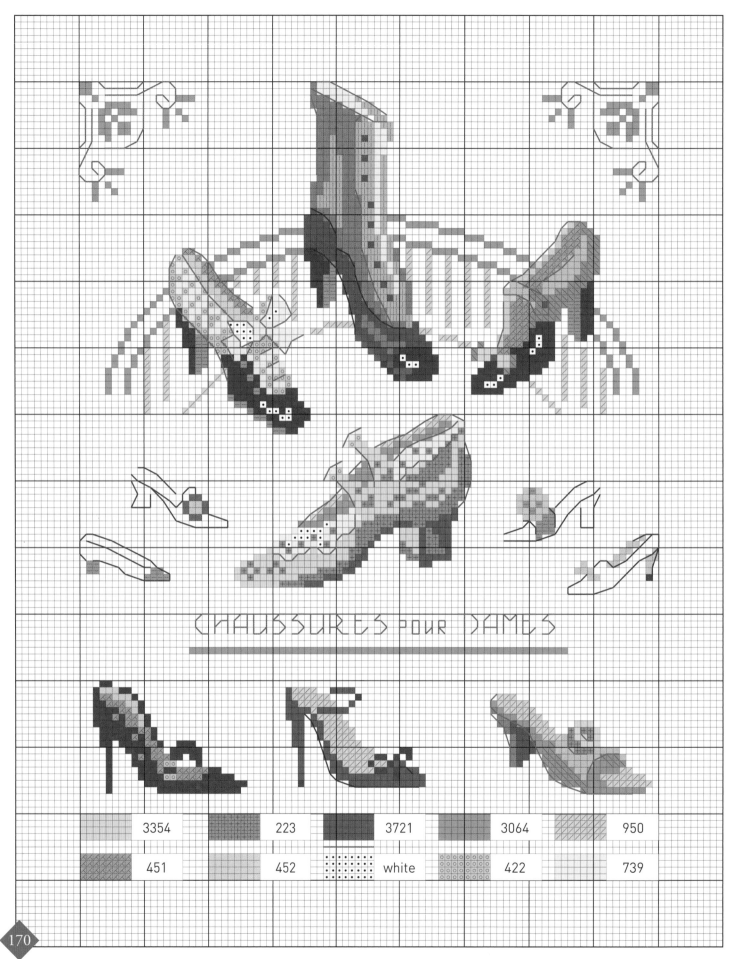

CHAUSSURES POUR DAMES

	3354		223		3721		3064		950
	451		452		white		422		739

A photo of the bottom designs is on page 167.

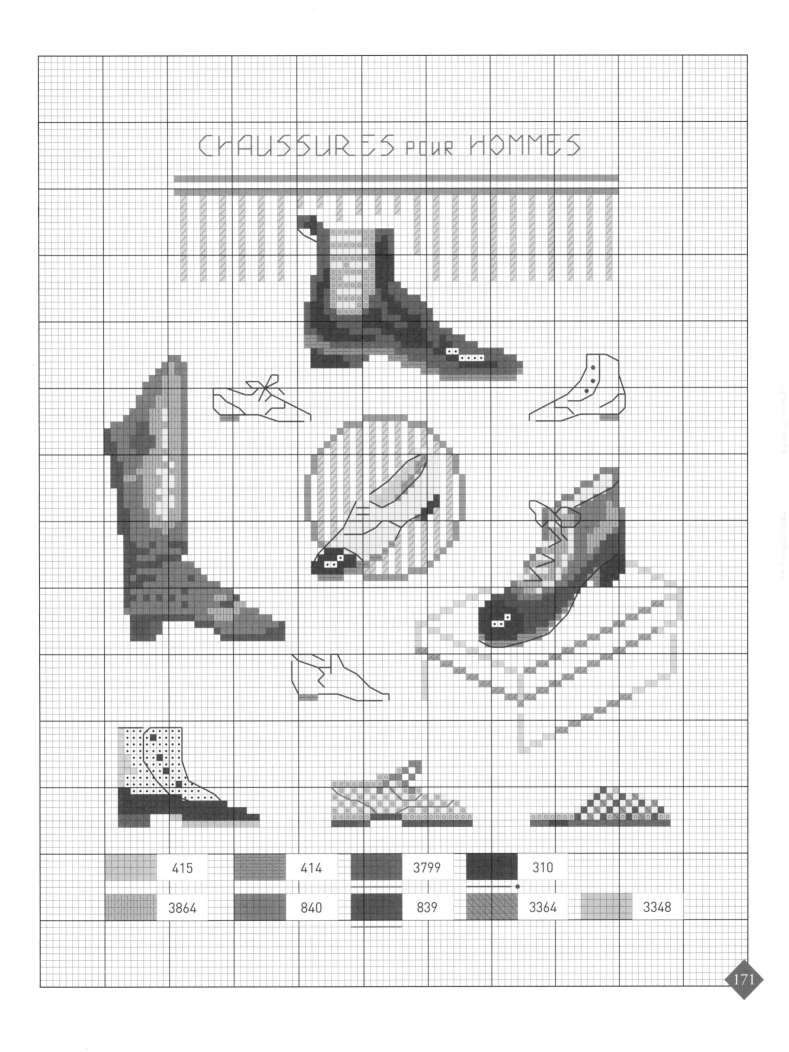

CHAUSSURES POUR HOMMES

	415		414		3799		310
	3864		840		839		3364		3348

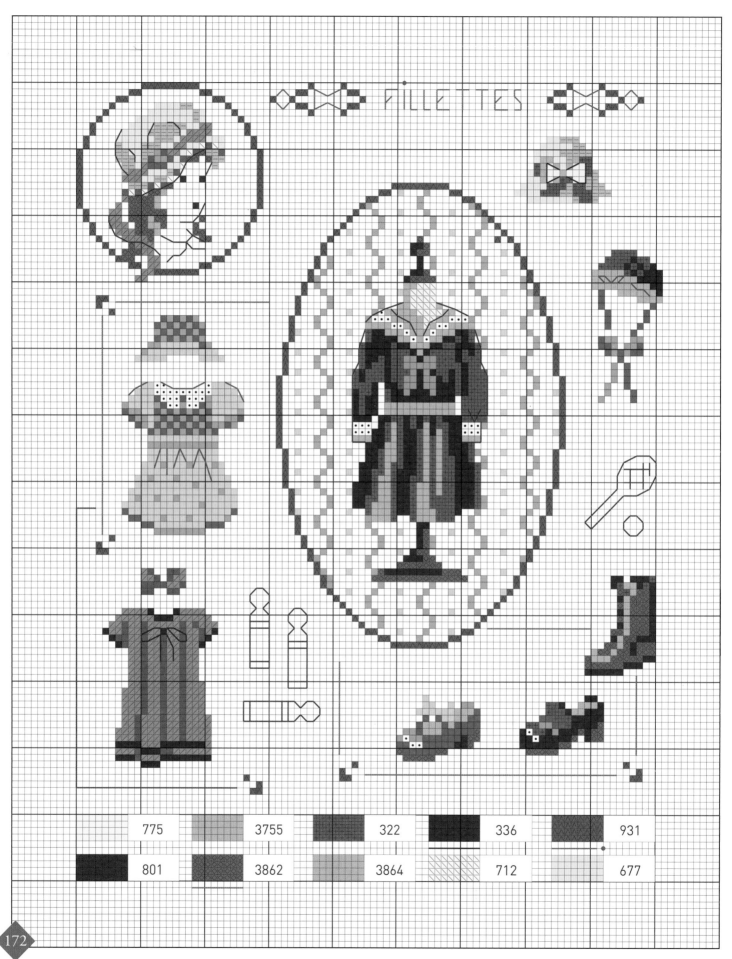

FILLETTES

	775		3755		322		336		931
	801		3862		3864		712		677

A photo of this design is on page 166.

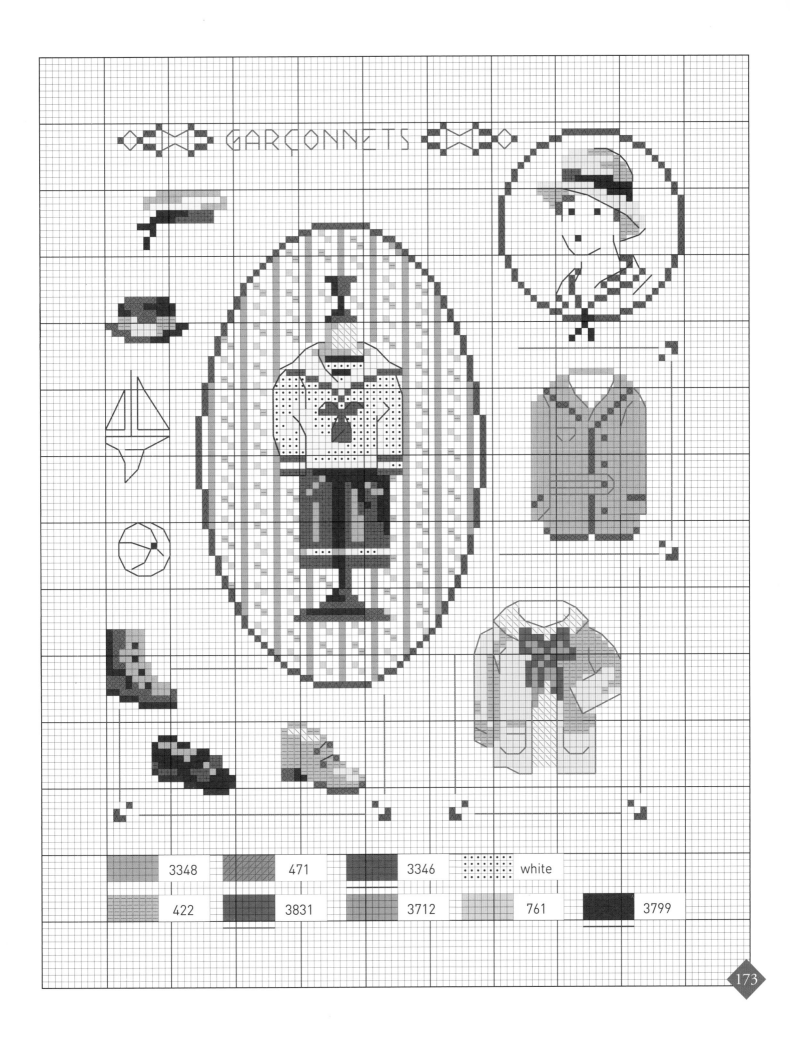

GARÇONNETS

	3348		471		3346		white
	422		3831		3712		761

	3799

ARTICLES de BAINS de MER

	white
	336
	312
	322
	3755
	775

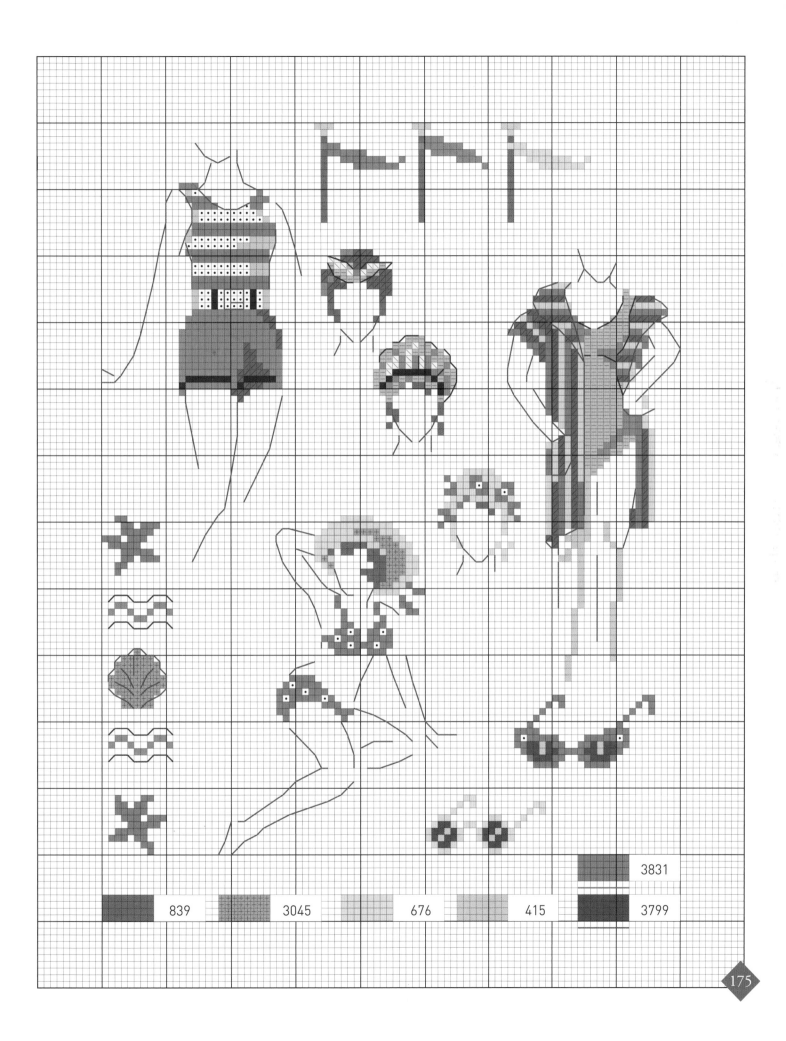

839 3045 676 415 3831 3799

175

	729		3829		434		3021
	3782		739		415		414		3799
	3803		3687		604		225		224

N°17

Collection Automne ~ Hiver

3755

322

3750

522

3790

841

842

225

3833

3831

3685

white

415

414

3799

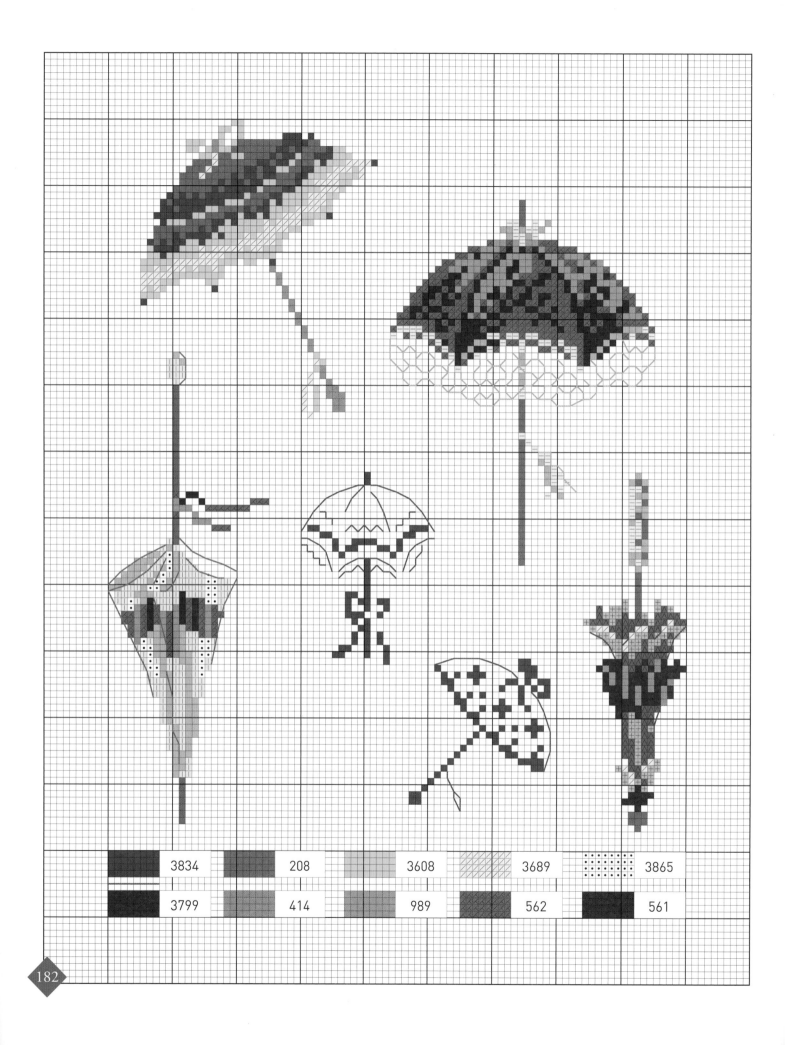

| | 3834 | | 208 | | 3608 | | 3689 | | 3865 |
| | 3799 | | 414 | | 989 | | 562 | | 561 |

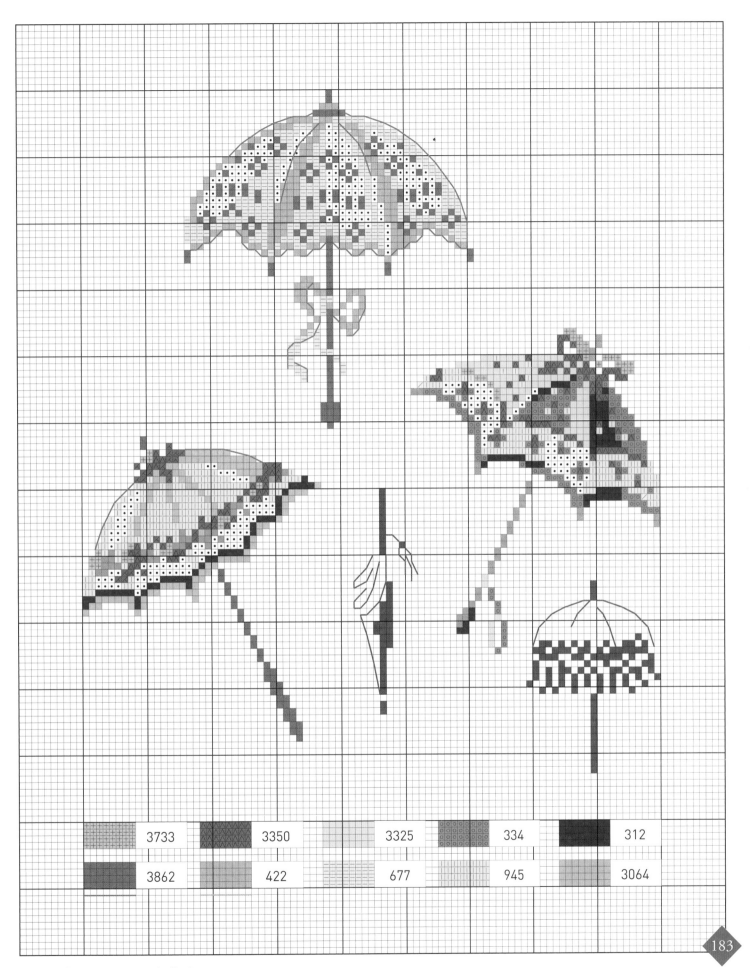

	3733		3350		3325		334		312
	3862		422		677		945		3064

A photo of the two center umbrellas is on page 179.

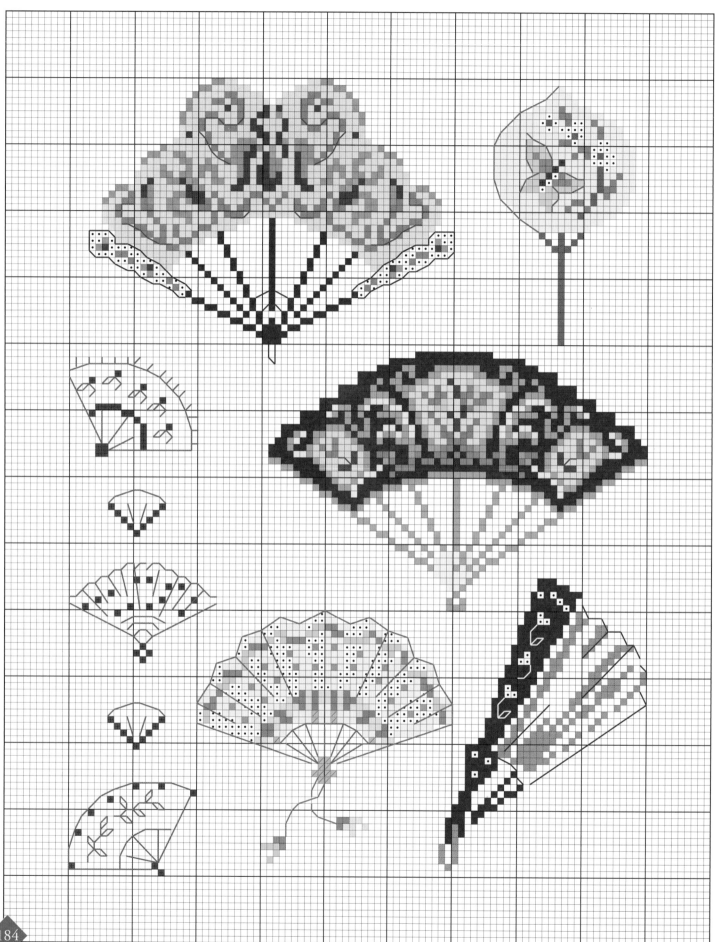

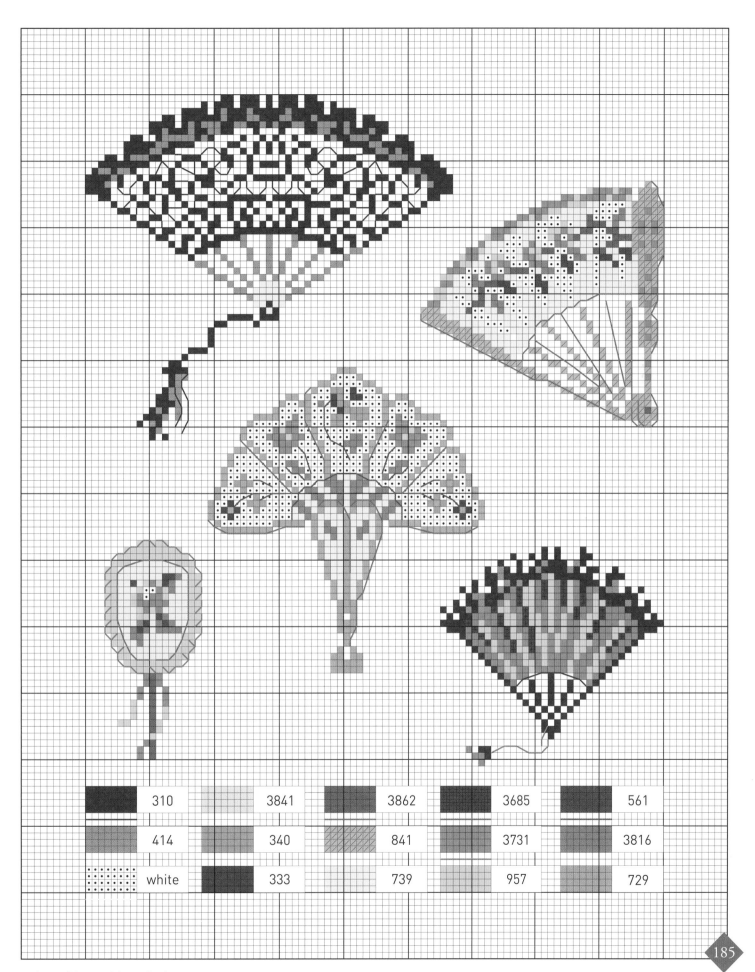

	310		3841		3862		3685		561
	414		340		841		3731		3816
	white		333		739		957		729

A photo of the top right design is on page 179.

	3803		3835		209		3864		3862
	739		422		168		169		535

A photo of this design is on page 178.

3865
3687
452
677
414
729
310
470

COMPTOIR DES CHEMISES

	839		840		3864		739
	3753		932		3768		367		368

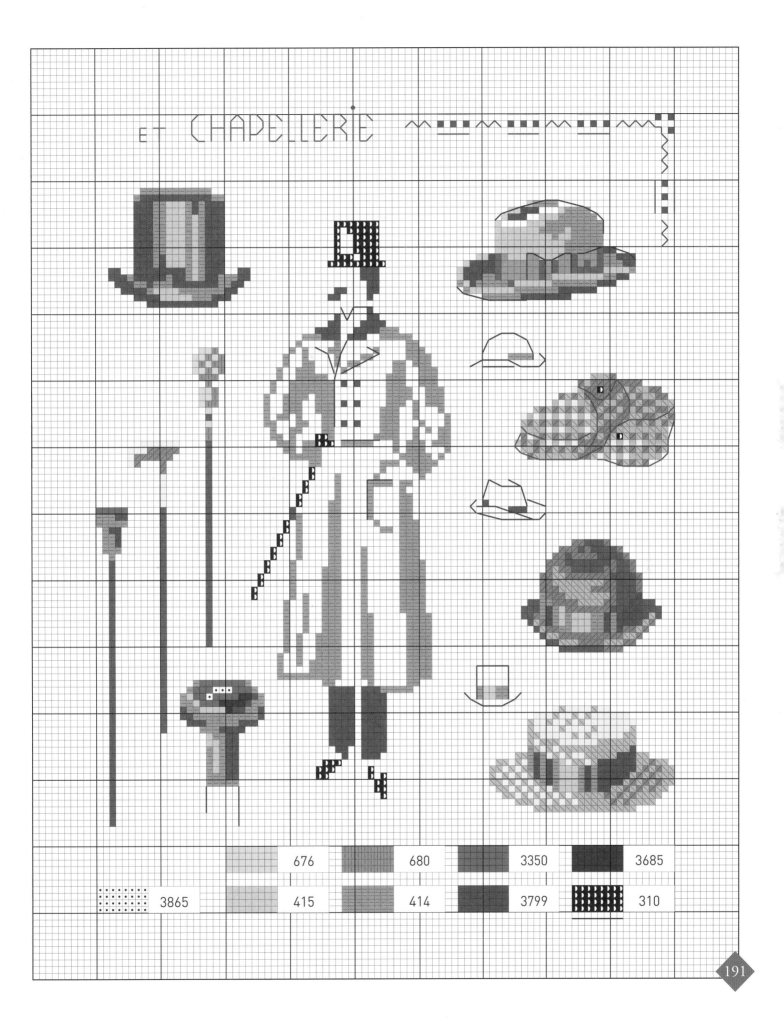

ET CHAPELLERIE

	676		680		3350		3685
3865		415		414		3799		310

Illustrator Véronique Enginger is the author of other books of cross stitch patterns including *Fables & Fairy Tales to Cross Stitch*. Her designs often focus on helping the charm of our memories enrich our current-day lives.